INTEGRATE THE SHADOW
MASTER YOUR PATH

Matthew B. James, MA, PhD

www.nlp.com

www.huna.com

INTEGRATE THE SHADOW
MASTER YOUR PATH

Matthew B. James, MA, PhD

ADVANCED NEURO DYNAMICS, INC.

75-6099 KUAKINI HIGHWAY HI KAILUA-KONA 96740

Balboa Press books may be ordered through booksellers or by contacting:

BALBOA.
PRESS
A DIVISION OF HAY HOUSE

Balboa Press
A Division of Hay House
1663 Liberty Drive
Bloomington, IN 47403
www.balboapress.com
1 (877) 407-4847

Because of the dynamic nature of the Internet, any web addresses or links contained in this book may have changed since publication and may no longer be valid. The views expressed in this work are solely those of the author and do not necessarily reflect the views of the publisher, and the publisher hereby disclaims any responsibility for them.

The author of this book does not dispense medical advice or prescribe the use of any technique as a form of treatment for physical, emotional, or medical problems without the advice of a physician, either directly or indirectly. The intent of the author is only to offer information of a general nature to help you in your quest for emotional and spiritual well-being. In the event you use any of the information in this book for yourself, which is your constitutional right, the author and the publisher assume no responsibility for your actions.

Any people depicted in stock imagery provided by Thinkstock are models, and such images are being used for illustrative purposes only.
Certain stock imagery © Thinkstock.

Cover image reproduced with permission of the http://earthref.org science web resource; photographer: Robert Petersen

Printed in the United States of America.

ISBN: 978-1-4525-8446-1 (sc)
ISBN: 978-1-4525-8445-4 (e)

Balboa Press rev. date: 3/5/2014

This book is dedicated to my son Ethan. Thank you for constantly teaching me what it means to be a good father. Every obstacle you have faced in your life has been handled with power and confidence and yet you have been able to keep a loving and caring spirit. I could not be more proud of you, and I am thankful you are my son.

TABLE OF CONTENTS

Foreword

We've taken charge in many aspects of our lives. We know we can improve our physical health by paying attention to what we eat, exercising, and resting our bodies and minds. Many of us no longer treat physicians as gods but as partners in our health, along with alternative health practitioners.

We know we can improve our personal lives by reducing stress, staying involved in positive relationships, pursuing our hobbies and interests. Many of us no longer stuff ourselves into the one-size-fits all lifestyle promoted by the media.

We know we can improve our spiritual connection by practices of meditation, silence, and by investigating to spiritual wisdom of the ages. Many of us no longer rely on individual gurus, priests, or preachers to show us our own true spiritual path.

And whether our focus is on more emotional, physical, or spiritual health and well-being, the key to our ability to effect any lasting change is within our unconscious minds.

An old myth used to claim that we only use 10% of our brains. We use all of our brains – but not consciously. A vast portion of the brain's activity is not conscious at all. It is in the realm of the unconscious mind, which is fully occupied by regulating our heartbeat and breathing, staying aware of danger in our environment, storing and organizing our memories, and filtering enormous amounts of input to determine what to bring to conscious awareness.

It's doing all of this and much more, without our conscious participation. Most of us know a little bit about it, but how many of us really understand how it works and how to work with it? We're all apparently equipped with this powerful apparatus called the unconscious, but we don't know how to consciously tap its power. In fact, sometimes it actually seems to be working at cross-purposes to what we really want.

Doesn't it feel like sometimes, even with our best intentions and strong conscious desire, we end up shooting ourselves in the foot? We eat what we swore we'd never eat again. We blow an exam even though we have studied and were confident about the material. We find ourselves attracted to the same destructive relationship even though we know better. We totally blank out on a deadline that is important to our business success. We fall asleep when we sit to meditate.

Psychoanalysts, psychologists and psychiatrists may spend years, even decades, studying the unconscious and how this powerful apparatus works for (and sometimes, against) us. But in INTEGRATE THE SHADOW, MASTER YOUR PATH, Dr. James breaks it down simply. He uses language that's easy to understand and gives illustrations that bring complex concepts down to earth.

Within the pages of this book, you'll come to understand:
• Why, at times, it appears that your unconscious urges are at odds with your conscious desires.

• How the beliefs held in your unconscious determine your decisions and color your perception of everything and everyone.

• What the most basic mission of your unconscious mind is and why you really want to honor it.

• How denying those dark urges of the Shadow can lead to sickness and failure.

• How the anima and animus housed in your unconscious will lead you to healthy or unhealthy relationships with the opposite sex.

- What part the unconscious plays on your spiritual path and in your relationship to Higher Self.

Throughout this book, you'll have those "aha" moments where you finally understand why you react the way you do to certain things, and why you've done some of the things you've done. More importantly, you'll know how you can work with your unconscious to produce different outcomes – whether it's in physical health, better relationships, career improvement, or spiritual growth. – Dr. Fab

Dr. Fabrizio Mancini is president emeritus of Parker University in Dallas, Texas, and a graduate of the Institute for Educational Management at Harvard University's Graduate School of Education. He is the bestselling author of The Power of Self-Healing and co-author of Chicken Soup for the Chiropractic Soul.

Dear Reader: I am honored to have Dr. Fab write the foreword of my book. Let me share some information about him so you can understand why we asked him to write a bit about the healing process. – Dr. Matt

Dr. Fabrizio Mancini is an internationally acclaimed wellness leader, educator, bilingual speaker and authority on self-healing. He is the author of the best-selling book, The Power of Self-Healing. A frequent guest of radio and television programs, he has been featured on Dr. Phil, The Doctors, FOX News, and numerous syndicated morning shows. Dr. Mancini has given testimony to the White House Commission for Complementary and Alternative Medicine and served on the Texas Governor's Advisory Council on Physical Fitness. His commitment to keeping the Hispanic community informed of healthy habits has led to numerous appearances on CNN Español, Univision, Telemundo, and Mundofox.

A native of Colombia, he immigrated to the US with his family at age 13. He became fluent in English as well as his native Spanish and went on to graduate from Parker University in Dallas, Texas, formerly known as Parker College of Chiropractic. After nine years in private practice, he became one of the youngest presidents of a college or university when he was chosen to lead Parker University in 1999. During his 13 years as President, he guided Parker University to historic educational and professional achievements. Dr. Mancini's tireless efforts to improve lives have been recognized with numerous honors, including Heroes for Humanity, Humanitarian of the Year, CEO of the Year, and induction into the Wellness Revolutionaries Hall of Fame. He recently was chosen as the namesake for the library at UNEVE, Mexico's new leading university. Dr. Mancini is also a graduate of the prestigious Institute for Educational Management in the Graduate School of Education at Harvard University. He is the author of Four Steps for Living a Fabulous Life, and co-author of Chicken Soup for the Chiropractic Soul and The Well Adjusted Soul. For more information, visit http://www.DrFabMancini.com.

OVERVIEW

In *Find Your Purpose, Master Your Path*, I compared the relationship of the conscious and unconscious minds to an orchestra. The conscious mind acts as the conductor, making sure the orchestra heads in the same direction to create the desired result. But the orchestra musicians themselves – our unconscious minds – provide all the energy, action and music. So it's important to understand how the unconscious works and how to work with it. Just as I used *Huna* and Jungian psychology as the basis to help you understand the workings of the conscious mind, I'll use them to describe the unconscious. Also, because practices in psychology such as hypnosis and NLP (Neuro Linguistic Programming) emphasize interaction with the unconscious, I'll draw on knowledge from those disciplines as well.

Western psychology and *Huna* see the unconscious mind similarly in many ways. Both acknowledge that the unconscious operates the body, synchronizing breathing and heartbeat, releasing hormones and regulating organ function without much input from the conscious mind. *Huna* and Western psychology also agree that the unconscious stores and organizes memories, which includes everything from remembering your own phone number to repressing memories associated with painful emotions.

But there are some differences. *Huna's* concept of the unconscious, the *unihipili*, is more general and does not make the distinctions that Jung thought were important. Also, many branches of Western psychology, and even some Jungians, view the unconscious almost as an adversary or as an uncivilized child who needs taming. Western spiritual paths and philosophies often teach that we should conquer this aspect of self or purify ourselves from it in order to attain higher levels of spirituality. But ancient Hawaiians respected the wisdom of their *unihipili* and their *na`au* (center or gut), appreciated its contribution to their well-being. They knew it played a critical role in the connection with higher self, which is more similar to the way Jung himself viewed the unconscious.

The literal translation of *unihipili* is "little creature" or "little one." If you see something scurrying across the floor you could say, "Oh, look! An *unihipili!*" The Hawaiians believed that the unconscious mind was a little self that lived inside you and they believed that the unihipili was wise and instrumental in keeping you both physically and emotionally healthy. They also saw the *unihipili* as the direct connection to Higher Self or Higher Consciousness, so it was important to treat it with respect. To trust the *na'au* (or center) is to be able to hear the messages from your unconscious intuition, from the *unihipili*.

GENERAL CHARACTERISTICS

The unconscious has many functions, such as running your physical systems, storing and organizing memories, maintaining instincts and generating habits. But to understand the unconscious, it's almost easier to think of the unconscious or *unihipili* as a "who" rather than a "what" because the unconscious has distinct characteristics and personality traits. The unconscious is similar to a 6 or 7 year old child in many ways. It is very literal, and it makes associations and absorbs learning quickly. For example, if it sees that a clever playmate is very popular, it might associate being smart with having friends. It might even conclude that if you are not smart, you will not have friends. Like a child, the unconscious wants to do a good job so it does its best to give you what it *thinks* you want and need. Following the prior example, it might feel desperate to do well in school so you are likeable. It functions best with simple, repetitive instruction, and the best thing you can do for your unconscious is to give it very clear marching orders to follow.

The unconscious also takes everything very personally so anything you say about another, your unconscious applies to itself. If you believe that "women can't be trusted" and you're a female, your unconscious may assume that you are untrustworthy as well. If you think people are strong in the face of adversity, your unconscious may assume that you will be strong in such circumstances too.

The unconscious is highly "moral," and just like a child, it totally buys into the morals in its environment. It absorbs and pretty much accepts at face value whatever that child's authority figures say is so. If Mom and Dad say that, "wealthy people are money grubbers," the unconscious believes that money is evil. If a child is rewarded for conforming and punished for being different, the unconscious knows that conformity is good and outside the box is bad.

Your unconscious communicates using emotion, symbols and images. It gives you butterflies and sweaty palms if it fears you'll be rejected when you ask that beautiful woman out. It sends you bizarre dreams to warn you not to take that job. It doesn't so much hear your words as it absorbs images of what you say, which explains why the unconscious does not process negatives easily. In goal setting and affirmations, you are always instructed to put your desires in the positive. Why? Because if you say, "I don't want to blow this interview," the image the unconscious absorbs is blowing the interview. The "not" part is lost. But if you set a goal of a "very successful interview," the unconscious has a definite picture and clear direction in how you want to be supported.

Another aspect of the unconscious is that it will always seek out the path of least resistance. When given many choices, the unconscious mind will seek out the shortest route from A to B. This aspect of the unconscious also gives rise to the idea that the simplest approach is more often the one we take. Is that always the case? No, but at the level of the unconscious mind, we like to KISS (Keep It Super Simple).

UNCONSCIOUS AND PROJECTION

As we discussed in *Find Your Purpose, Master Your Path*, everything is your projection because you're only going to see 126 bits out of the possible 2,000,000 bits per second, of anything you perceive. If you compare notes after a couple of years to someone else who attended an event with you, your experience of the event will be vastly different than that other person's, which means your perception was your projection of what's going on. It's the job of the unconscious to filter through the billion bits of data coming at you to determine which 126 bits you'll notice. And those 126 bits can determine the course of your life. The unconscious bases this filtering system on its beliefs and attitudes, many of which are not conscious at all. But by bringing these unconscious beliefs to the surface, you can modify the filters of your unconscious.

For example, if your unconscious holds the belief that you are unattractive to the opposite sex, you will never notice someone who signals that they'd like to get to know you. Or if your unconscious is convinced that you are brilliant, you may never notice your own mistakes. Unconscious beliefs are not intrinsically good or bad. The point is that you want to uncover them and maybe balance them so you can be consciously empowered.

THE SHADOW

"Everything that irritates us about others can lead to a deeper understanding of ourselves." – Carl Jung

THE SHADOW APPEARS

My daughter Skylar was about a year and a half old. We were walking around the house and walked past a wall. Suddenly Skylar stopped and looked over at the wall. She moved her arm and, out of my peripheral vision, I saw her shadow moving. She moved her other arm. And all of a sudden, she jumped back. "Daddy, what's that?" "That's your shadow." "Whoa."

Skylar spent most of the next three or four days looking for walls where she could see her shadow, play with her shadow, and get to know her shadow. In the beginning, she was afraid of her shadow. She tried to run away from it. She was very concerned at one point: Why was it connected to her feet? She looked underneath her feet to see if anything was there, but when she leaned over, the shadow seemed to be connected to her butt! It was a wonderful experience!

Do you remember that? Being afraid of your shadow when you first became aware of it? Well, as adults, when we first become aware of our internal Shadow self, it's very frightening. And I think this initial fear happens because in the early phases of our lives (what Jung calls the first half of our lives), a lot of the focus is on developing a healthy ego, learning who we are in the world, learning who to be *externally*.

The world, the external, is glamorous when you're a young adult. Your ego is developing and the ego gets fed by the world. Ah, that purse, that job, that title, that degree, that girlfriend. You go out to get that whatever it is, which is very ego-driven. Jung referred to the first half of being life as very ego-driven, and appropriately so. What is the first half of life? Jung picked the age of around 29 or 30, which might seem arbitrary. Astrologers wouldn't say it's arbitrary though; it's the period leading up to your first Saturn return.

We usually use that first 29 or 30 years to develop a healthy ego. We become confident in ourselves. We get on top of our game, successful and confident. We're pretty sure of who and what we are. But then all of a sudden, according to Jung, you hear and feel that uncomfortable rattling around in the corner. Out of nowhere just when you think you've got it all together, the Shadow appears. And unless you resolve that Shadow, it continues to rattle, agitate and irritate.

The Shadow appears just when you think you're really something or someone. Just about the time you feel like you're pretty special, like you've got it down. Do you remember that point where you thought, "Ah man, I am the dudette. I've got it down." Suddenly, wham! The Shadow appears when we least expect it.

As humans, we don't seem to have a lot of ability to anticipate the Shadow. I've had students email me and ask, "When should we expect the Shadow?" When you least expect it. Jung's idea about personal development is that you develop a healthy ego in the first half of life. You become able to function outside in the world with some personal satisfaction. Then he said that the second half of life is about turning away from the outer world and looking deeply inside.

So, in the first 29-30 years, you've figured out how to present a persona. You've got an ego, healthy or not. Now it's time to dive into your internal self and find out what's going on inside there. This is part of the path to individuation or self-actualization. And for this part of the path, one of the first places to investigate is the Shadow.

SHADOW DEFINED

Let me give you a simple definition of what the Shadow is. The Shadow is all that you think is not you. See, once you have fully defined who and what you are, by the very nature of the assumption of creation[1], all that you are *not* also comes into existence. That existence is defined in the form of the Shadow. It's the not-me. It is the qualities that we deny in ourselves. The Shadow arrives or becomes an issue when a person is purely persona-focused or ego-driven.

The Shadow is everything that we do not accept as being in the self. "I would not do that. That is not me. I am not that way." In my book about conscious mind, *Find Your Purpose, Master Your Path*, I used an example of the dad who yells at his kids after a frustrating day at work, then blames them for his behavior rather than recognizing his own short fuse. Based on Jung's Shadow concept, it is possible that this same person may be a big advocate for treating children with respect or maybe is adamantly against violence. "I am totally against unkind behavior. That is not me."

In this case, the man has to make excuses for his not-me behavior when he becomes his Shadow, the "mean" self that he can't cop to. It becomes a natural act of projection. "It's not me, so it must be those darn kids who need disciplining!"

The Shadow begins to appear when we have confined ourselves into the box that is the ego or the persona we show to the world. Prior to meeting our Shadow, life is very one-dimensional. "I'm a banker." "I'm a trainer." "I'm a husband." "I'm a wife." That's a very one-dimensional life. Do you remember when your role or title was all important? People would ask, "What do you do?" "I run The Empowerment Partnership. I'm the president of the company." Very one-dimensional. This is what I do. This is who I am.

---

1 *The law of creation states that whenever something is created, its direct opposite is created at the same time.*

As we develop and define our own ego, we can also become one-dimensional emotionally. "I'm very responsible." "I'm open-minded." "I'm loving." Really? *Always?*

Deep down inside, we know life is more than that. Deep down inside, we realize that we are more than just that one-dimensional being. And that's really when the Shadow begins to appear and show itself.

I love a quote I saw from Amy Grant: "Without black, no color has any depth. But if you mix black with everything, suddenly there's shadow - no, not just shadow, but fullness. You've got to be willing to mix black into your palette if you want to create something that's real."

The ego casts the Shadow. And just as you don't want to get rid of the ego because it has an important purpose, the idea is not to get rid of your Shadow. The Shadow has an important purpose too. Any book that says the Shadow is evil, dirty or nasty and should be eliminated has been written by someone who is projecting it out because it's something *they* have repressed. They're still at the "It's not me" stage.

IT'S IN ALL OF US

You may have heard of the Milgram Studies that originated at Yale University. In the '60s, Yale University psychologist Stanley Milgram began studying the atrocities that occurred during World War II. His basic question was, "How can something like this happen? How can people of good conscience harm that many individuals?" Milgram's initial hypothesis was that there must be something wrong with the Germans. (I mean no offense by this, just stating what he thought. Besides if this bothers you, great! This is the right chapter for you! Keep reading!) Originally, he intended to conduct a study in the U.S. then go to Germany and conduct the exact same study to prove that we, here in the U.S., would never do anything so uncivilized.

Wouldn't most of us say that, no matter what our nationality? "*We* would never do such a horrible thing."

Milgram set up an experiment. He sent several subjects, let's call them Person A, into a room where they looked through a one-way mirror at another person, Person B, who was strapped up to electrodes. Person B was supposed to give correct answers to certain questions. If they didn't give the right answer, Person A was to hit a button that would give Person B a shock.

By the way, Person B was an actor or another psychologist who was in on the study. The study wasn't about Person B, although Person A was told that the study was all about Person B. Person A thought they were just helping out.

Person B was instructed to give the wrong answer every time, no matter what. Person A had a button to hit to give Person B a shock, but they also had a dial that supposedly regulated the strength of the shock. The dial had numbers and clear labels that said "minor shock" or "mild shock," "intense shock," "severe shock," and "warning: can cause severe harm." After that point, the numbers were not labeled, clearly to show, if you go past this, you're really going to fry Person B's eggs!

So Person B would give the wrong answer. Person A was told to take it up to the first setting and hit the button and they did as they told. were Person B gave the next wrong answer, and Person A was told to take the shock up to the next setting. Hit the button. Person A would do it. Wrong answer and up to the next setting, they'd raise the setting and push the button again. Some of the subjects who were Person A began to protest, "They're screaming in pain in there. I don't want to do this." But Milgram would say, "You have to do this. Don't worry. They're not really being harmed." Nearly 100 percent of the Person A's took the dial *past the warning point*! Some Person B's even pretended they passed out, and Milgram would say, "Hit it again."

Even then, Person A would almost always hit the shock button again.

Think about it: these were people of good conscience, good-minded individuals, a random sample that could have included you or me. But they all did something that might make you squeamish even just to read about it. By the way, Milgram did not take the study to Germany at that point. He concluded exactly what Carl Jung said quite some time ago: that *we all carry inside us the potential of that thing that we say we would never do or become.*

Interestingly, Milgram denied that he himself would ever have taken the dial past the warning point. But, as a very astute Jungian psychologist named Robertson pointed out, Milgram did act cruelly during his experiment by forcing Person A to continue and letting them believe they were harming someone. He clearly understood that everyone was going overboard, yet continued the experiment for the sake of science.

So you see, even Milgram, ego-driven in the name of science, became the Shadow. He became similar to the actual people who had commanded others to commit atrocities and kill millions of human beings during World War II. He himself became the Shadow[2]. Even though he did not go to the same extreme, he did cross the line.

Another study in 1971 looked at a similar question. In this one, Stanford psychology professor Philip Zimbardo enlisted a group of college students who were then screened. He chose twenty-four who tested as the most psychologically stable and healthy, then randomly assigned twelve of them to be prisoners and twelve to be prison guards. The basement of a university building was retrofitted as a mock prison, and prisoners and guards were even dressed in appropriate uniforms.

Though the experiment was scheduled to last for two weeks, it was called off after only 6 days. Within a day, the prisoners had completely taken on the role of being a prisoner, some even becoming suicidal.

----

2 *But by the way, because of these studies, all universities adopted Institutional*
Review BVdards, which are designed to ensure subject safety in experiments like these.

Likewise, the guards quickly began to abuse the prisoners both psychologically and physically. As healthy as they had appeared to be, these psychologically stable and healthy subjects just slipped right into their roles. That's called the Shadow.

Why am I pointing this out? Because anytime you say, "That's not me. I could never do it," I want to point out that it is within you. And as scary as that may sound, the Shadow is something you do need to acknowledge and reconcile. Even for the most peace-loving activist, there are countless instances of harm being done for the sake of the cause. Personally, as peaceful as you are, if someone you loved was being threatened and in danger, I'm betting you'd find a violent urge inside yourself that would make Rambo look like a wimp.

Jung says the Shadow is that which is not in consciousness and, because it is not in consciousness, it must be projected out onto the world around us. Okay, so let's do the math. If 90 percent of who you are is unconscious, then 90 percent of who you are must be projected. We think we have a unique identity when we look in the mirror. We think we would never do or feel or say things that we find disgusting or abhorrent. But when we look out at the world, we are looking at all that we are at the unconscious level.

COUNTER BALANCE TO BALANCE

Who we think we are – our roles, our personality, our conscious preferences – is the ego. Therefore, everything we think we are *not* gets projected and/or thrown into the Shadow. By the very nature of how things work, that self-regulating system of balance, the not-us is thus projected around us as our experience of our reality or the world.

Here's the easiest way to think of the Shadow: the Shadow is the equal and opposite reaction to the personality. Ego is the sum total of your personality. The Shadow is the equal and opposite reaction to the personality.

So according to Jung, if we are extroverted, the Shadow would be introverted. If we are intuitive (processing information through our "sixth sense"), the Shadow is a sensor (processing information through the five senses only). If we're kind, the Shadow is cruel. If we are open-minded, the Shadow is intolerant. The Shadow is always a counterbalancing position to the personality.

A student once asked me a very good question: Is it the Higher Self that seeks this balance? The answer is no. The Higher Self is already balanced by its very nature. Therefore balance is not the role of the Higher Self. Balance is the role of the unconscious. The unconscious seeks balance for the conscious ego and personality, thus projects the Shadow to balance the energies because it's the unconscious mind's job to transmit, distribute and flow energy.

The Law of Balance is simple: it states that the universe seeks a balance and/or harmony in most of its aspects. Think of moving from winter to summer. At a point in the middle you have balance called the equinox. Just like nature, we have internal energies that need to be balanced. The opposite of internal is external. Therefore, think of the external as a balancer for the internal.

Even though each of us has a life path that is unique, in all of us, our unconscious mind pushes us towards *wholeness*. Rather than thinking of balance as in nature, maybe it's clearer to say that the unconscious mind's push towards wholeness is what causes it to project the Shadow.

According to Jung, there is no psychological extreme which cannot, in a moment, flip to the opposite side. A man who has a total lack of confidence may project that people all around him are extremely confident. His Shadow is confident, so he perceives confidence in others, and falls into situations where others' confidence is called for and where they express that confidence. And he could also have a strong abreaction to it, viewing others' confidence negatively as vain, narcissistic, or cocky. Or, on the flip side, he could view all of these confident others as superior to himself.

I really like psychological extreme examples in people. For example, people who advocate doing no harm for their entire lives. "You can't kill people." They take up a cause and target abortion clinic doctors as "murderers." Then, in extreme cases, a person could even end up killing one of these "murderers." They become the very thing they stand against.

Gandhi, one of the world's most revered peacemakers and advocates for non-violence, confessed to being abusive to his wife in his younger years. More than one Bible-quoting minister has practiced the "sinful" adultery he railed against. Good guys are exposed as bad guys everyday – and vice versa. As Jung said, "Every extreme psychological position has the potential to flip into its opposite." And this flip is a lot easier than you imagine.

The farther we are away from a balance point in our lives, the more we can expect a dramatic flip. The farther we are from a balance point in a given situation or context, the more we can expect that we will flip into its opposite. Every extreme conscious position secretly contains its opposite.

There is a real danger in holding a rigid belief system that the world is one way and only one way. If we perceive the world as this one way, everything fits into nice, tidy, clear-cut categories. We divide the world into clear-cut opposites and embrace one side. It's good versus evil. "I'm going to be good. And that means, by God, that I'll be happy. There are mean people and nice people. I will be nice."

Off the top, that doesn't sound too bad, right? Who can argue with being nice? But the more we rigidly attempt to be nice to everyone, the more likely it is that someone who is rude or selfish will come into our awareness. Have you ever been so rigidly positioned on being polite or nice to someone, only to have him or her simply spit in your face? Nice versus rude is a great example. "I'm going to make a conscious effort. I'm going to be nice to everyone I meet." Within a matter of moments, you're meeting someone who's completely rude and brash. The unconscious mind has to do that. The unconscious mind figures, "Okay. If you embrace one side consciously, if you so consciously dig your heels in and embrace this, I've got to spotlight the jerks out there. It's a self-regulating system. So you go ahead and be Mr. Nice Guy and I'll show you the jerks."

Let me give you a personal example. In my practitioner trainings, I'll swear occasionally as I'm talking on stage to loosen people up. It makes the atmosphere more casual and lets people know it's okay to just be who they are there. But during one training, apparently I got a little carried away. After the session, some of the attendees made comments that my swearing was too much. I asked my wife Soomi about it and she said, "You know I love you and I don't mind your swearing. But you sounded like one of those hip hop guys who can't think of any other word besides the F-bomb. Maybe you could tone it down." So I thought about it. I had a Master Practitioners' course coming up and I decided I wasn't going to swear at all. I was going to cut all swearing out completely and be squeaky clean. I thought it would be easy, especially since I was co-teaching with another trainer named Topher Morrison who rarely swears at all.

But from our first moment on stage, Topher took off. I'd say something like, "Gosh, I love NLP." And Topher would chime in with "F*** yeah! NLP is f***ing awesome!" Every time he swore, I'd physically flinch. Finally, at one of the breaks, I turned off my mic and said to him, "What the heck is wrong with you? You're swearing like a drunken sailor!" He shrugged and said, "I don't know. That sh*t just keeps popping out."

So the training continued and, in talking about past life regression, I said, "For this exercise, please don't choose some awful experience.

That isn't the purpose. Choose a happy time." Topher immediately chimed in with, "Yeah, we don't want to hear 'Oh, I was a urinal biscuit in a past life and everyone was pissing on me.'" I couldn't believe he said that!

With only 3 days left in the training, a guy walked out of the training and handed Soomi a note as he left. Basically it said, "The reason I'm leaving is that Matt's constant use of profanity makes the environment intolerable. I'm requesting a refund but I'd be happy to see Topher in a future training." Me?!?

That is absolutely classic textbook Jung Shadow. I was reacting and rejecting my own Shadow. I took an extreme position on something and immediately had to project the opposite out onto someone else and bear the consequences of being so rigid. Papa Bray said, "The enlightened *kahuna* can hold two conflicting truths in mind without it creating any conflict." As soon as I let go of any conflict of whether or not I'd swear, students stopped having issues with it.

By the way, the Shadow does not appear to make us throw out our current belief system and values. The Shadow doesn't have any judgment about either end of any spectrum. It doesn't show up to say, "Matt, throw out that belief that you shouldn't swear." It just wants to balance things out, to bring you to wholeness. The Shadow, with its not-you, appears so we may discover that our current set of values and beliefs are too restricted. It doesn't care whether you adopt them or not. It just wants to point out you're being a positional putz.

The more rigid you are in that belief system, the more positional you are, the farther you are away from the balancing point, the bigger the expression of the Shadow has to be. By that very nature of your extreme position, you are taking and putting more weight on one end of the seesaw. So the unconscious mind has to be more extreme and put more weight on the opposite side of the seesaw in the form of the Shadow. If you determine that you will only think positive thoughts for example, your unconscious will develop super negative beliefs to balance you out. If you claim to be cool and unflappable, your unconscious will seek out awkward, embarrassing situations to put you in.

To operate in the world, you have to develop an ego. But as soon as you say, "This is the boundary, this is my ego," then that which you are *not*, by its very nature, becomes unconscious. Anything that you are not consciously aware of becomes unconscious. In order to create balance, the unconscious mind has to place those unconscious qualities out there as the Shadow. If this is you, if this is me, that's the not-me. The Shadow is everywhere and it's all around you.

Have you ever seen girls who want to play with Tonka trucks or mechanical things and they're told not to? Or boys who want to play with stuffed animals but are shamed out of it? When my daughter Skylar got into Spiderman and started wanting Spiderman stuff rather than like Hello Kitty things, I got her Spiderman Crocs. She was Spiderman for a while.

We didn't say, "No, you can't do that. You're a girl." See, those qualities don't go away. Jung felt that the qualities we have denied in our life don't disappear completely. Instead, they hide out for a while and become part of the Shadow. They become unconscious and forgotten. The qualities we've denied become personified in the Shadow.

The fact is that many little girls are turned away from their mechanical interests because it's not a "feminine" trait. By the time a girl is an adult, she may have forgotten her desire to work with things mechanical. But one day she finds a dilemma she can't solve with her present, non-mechanical resources. So the Shadow might first show up in her dreams, and she might dream about mechanical things. According to Jung, if she integrates mechanical abilities into her personality, then the Shadow appearing in her dreams might become more human and more personal. As she begins to accept this quality and integrate it into her own persona or ego, she will feel less out of balance.

Jungians believe that the Shadow figure appears in dreams virtually every night. But the extreme nightmarish ones only appear when something has gone wrong with the process, when you have become too rigid in a certain aspect. You're far off your path. When you're too ego-driven and restricted, denying an aspect of yourself, the Shadow first appears in your dreams as nightmarish. You wake up feeling awful and thinking that your world is going to end.

In Jungian psychology, frequent nightmares are a clear indication of unresolved Shadow-related issues. Take the example of the girl who was not allowed to do mechanical things and rejected the mechanical side of herself. The Shadow might first appear in her dream as a huge mechanical robot hell-bent on destroying her town. Jungians would encourage her to journal about her dreams, question them, reflect on them. By doing so, they believe she could get closer to reconciling that "mechanical" side of herself. And as she does, her dreams would become more personal. She might find herself tinkering with a machine that seems wounded or a mechanical object may speak to her and give her an important insight.

In Jungian psychology, therapists encourage you to journal about your dreams to get closer to the issues they represent. As you get closer to resolution of these issues, the Shadow you are projecting into your dreams will feel more personified. As it becomes more human, it's easier to work with. Something nightmarish makes you want to get away from it. "I don't want to deal with it. I don't want to work with it. That's too scary." Something that is more human, as opposed to nightmarish, is easier.

But easy or hard, the fact is that the Shadow is not going to go away.

CREATING THE ENEMY

As soon as the lightness splits off from the darkness and you identify with the light, anyone who is not in the light is in the dark. So if there are good and evil people, anyone who is not identified as good, by that very concept, must then be evil. If you're either good or evil, the unconscious mind, by that very nature, has to project the other side out. The truth is that we need the values that are hidden in the Shadow, as much as we need the values that we hold to the light.

In discussing this part of Jung's work, Dr. Robin Robertson in the book *The Beginner's Guide to Jungian Psychology*, said that we look at our enemies and we see everything that we do not want to have in ourselves. And in extreme examples, we want to destroy that enemy. The child who hasn't developed his intellect wants to destroy the smart kid. The person who has been rigid in their diet might believe that anyone who does not eat exactly as they eat cannot be spiritual. The Shadow is being projected out to create an "enemy."

I remember a time when I was with my friend and fellow trainer David Shephard. He and I were eating lunch during a break in the training when a new student walked up and said, "Matt, Dave. I'm sorry to interrupt your lunch but I have a quick question." Suddenly she looked appalled when she saw the New York strip steak on Dave's plate. "You're eating meat?" With a mouthful of half-chewed meat, he looked up at her and said, "Yeah." She looked at me and said, "I want a refund. Clearly you guys aren't spiritual."

I don't want to arbitrarily pick on vegans so let me give you a counter example. Have you ever met someone who's gone so far down the Atkins path that if you even look at a carb, if you even think of a carb, they insist you're on the road to obesity and disease? If you're an Atkins devotee, my wife Soomi can absolutely help out with any Shadow issues you have. As soon as you go down that road with her, she'll order her favorite lunch: "I would like a chocolate block with chocolate dips on the side. Oh yeah, and I'd like some brown rice with that. Make it white rice."

So it's a very typical experience of the Shadow that we see and react to the enemy. In fact that's the first step toward resolution: You see the Shadow. You recognize that it's outside you. "That's not me. That's the enemy." So literally, if you are at a point on the path where you are seeing the not-you, that's a great place to be. Acknowledging that projection is the first step - recognizing that you do actually have the Shadow.

I ran into a personal example of this many years ago before I started teaching. I attended a seminar my father gave and he was saying that, in ancient times in Hawai'i, sexual acts weren't seen as evil, dirty, or nasty. Someone in the group asked something specifically about sexual assault and rapes. Out of the blue, I felt my blood boil. Anger at something that is totally out of proportion to the situation is a Shadow response. It is absolutely an indicative symbol experience of the Shadow just coming to life.

After the seminar, my father came up to me and said, "You look really fried. What the heck's going on?" I said, "I don't know. What you said just so bothered me. And it's not you. It's clearly me." I was at the stage where I recognized that it was me, my issues and not the projections I placed on others. I said, "You know, it's so bizarre. I can be watching TV and channel surfing, and I'll find a show in which there's a rape victim, fictitious or real. There's a newscast about someone who was just sexually assaulted. I mean, I just lose it."

I knew I needed to reconcile this. So I talked it through with my father. "How could it possibly fit as a Shadow projection? Did it mean that deep down inside somewhere I wanted to rape someone?" But my father just smiled and said, "No. It's never that simple. I've seen the respect you have for your mom, your partner, and women in general. But there is something, obviously, or it wouldn't come up."

A lot of people avoid believing that their perception is a Shadow projection because they think, "I see that but how can that be me? That's not me." It's ugly and grotesque to you, but what you truly have to realize is at some deeper level, it is you. As the Stanford and Yale psychological studies have shown, though we believe we can't be like that awful person we see, given the right circumstance, it is actually quite possible that we act out what we think is horribly evil.

So I did a lot of soul-searching on this one. It was around the time when I was beginning to reconcile my Shadow in relationships. Suddenly, it dawned on me that, in the relationship I was in at the time, I had no freedom of expression within our intimacy. I had no freedom to say, "Here's what I enjoy. Here's what I don't enjoy." I felt almost a shame and a fear, a fear that translated into anger, about expressing who and what I was. (Oddly enough, after the two of us were no longer together, my partner told me she had felt the exact same way.)

My Shadow, to bring this conflict up into my experience, put the most extreme of what I am *not* out there in front of me. It might seem easier to ignore it. To not look at it rather than to truly critically look at yourself and say, "If this is bothering me so much, what do I need to know?" But if you don't ask and investigate, you need to construct tighter and tighter defenses against the Shadow's messages. Like the politicians who make big speeches about the sanctity of marriage while secretly yearning for affairs: the longer they ignore the symbol of that yearning, the stronger the Shadow becomes until they find themselves acting out what they claim to stand against.

Rape and sexual violence were symbols to me, which had a strong emotional hook. What I had to do was be courageous. Carl Jung said, "A person on the path of individuation has to have courage and be courageous to face that which we think is so much not us." You have to face whatever it is but when you reconcile it, you realize, "Well, of course. Of course that amount of violence (or whatever it is) is not in me." No, violence toward women was not what I was holding in my heart. Yet, the imbalance in intimacy in my relationship was really bothering me. There just wasn't a tender intimacy in my relationship, and I couldn't even express to my partner that I needed that tenderness. That sometimes I just wanted a hug. It was very simple. But I so denied who and what I was, and what I wanted, that it had to burst out somehow. The extreme of the Shadow response is related to the level of denial not the extreme nature of what is being denied.

FIRST PHASE: SEEING THE ENEMY

So back to the swearing story: I took a strong position, "I'm not going to swear anymore." So the first thing I do is I recognize that Topher is swearing. That's the stage of seeing your Shadow, becoming conscious of the external projection, the not-me. Some Jungians call it "the enemy" and it may feel like the enemy because a lot of people encounter an extreme not-me or Shadow to balance some extreme position they've taken.

At this phase, where you are just seeing the Shadow, you are absolutely seeing it as it's totally outside. It's not-me. Some textbooks on Jungian psychology call this "the crusader phase" because when you see it out there and you have that desire to squash it. You want to destroy it because it reminds you of what you should not be or don't want it to be.

In phase one, the Shadow is outside of you, and this phase is characterized by the emotion of fear. Anger is also possible, as a mask to the fear. Jung believed that you knew you had Shadow issues if you had fear or anger. A great example is when you meet someone that you've never, ever met before. As soon as you meet them, you're thinking, "I don't like this person. There is just something about them I don't like." If that's where you are, you're at stage one. The enemy is not you. It's way outside.

When you have a hook or strong position, remember that the ego will always cast the Shadow. When there is a Shadow imbalance or a problem, you have not yet integrated your Shadow, that hook is going to be fear or anger. How do you know you need to work on the Shadow? A fear or anger response to an external projection, especially a person of the same sex and your immediate response is, "I don't like that person." (If you're reacting to someone of the opposite sex, it may deal with anima / animus which we cover later in this book). Any subcategory of anger like irritation or annoyance, in my humble opinion and based on *Huna*, points to a Shadow issue. It's just not as extreme. At the extreme, you have anger or fear reaction.

In the first stage, there can be a denial: "That's not really there. It doesn't exist." To avoid facing the Shadow, you try to delete it from your awareness. You may pretend to not be afraid or angry about it. Have you ever pretended to not be angry with someone that you just wanted to choke? That's phase one.

As long as we stay in the first stage, by the way, we have no hope of dealing with the Shadow. Across the board, Jungian textbooks that say if you continue to remain in that first stage, "that's not me," you can't resolve the Shadow. Especially if you actively fight against it, become a crusader: "Let's go get those bad guys. I'm going to make my life about making those people miserable."

That may seem like a virtuous thing to do but have you ever met someone who absolutely takes up a crusade? "Here is what I stand for. I am against this. And I'm going to go after it." They just get angrier and more adamant and maybe even deny that they're angry. They may project their anger on to the enemy. Jung said that if you live in that first phase, the not-me stage, self-righteously hanging on to anger or fear, it builds up and it doesn't allow you to get closer to resolution.

Mother Teresa was pretty smart about the Shadow. Most people would think of her as a strong pacifist. But she said, "I was once asked why I don't participate in anti-war demonstrations. I said that I will never do that, but as soon as you have a pro-peace rally, I'll be there." She had figured out that being "anti" something doesn't work, doesn't resolve the Shadow. As George Foreman once said, "I've seen George Foreman shadow boxing and the shadow won."

Now if you've been in some spiritual practice or in therapy or if you are one of my *Huna* students, you may have let go of a lot of anger, sadness, fear and guilt. You may feel it less. However, no matter how you feel it, this is not a conscious process. The Shadow comes from the unconscious and is resolved in the unconscious. The barometer is your feelings. If you begin to over-think it or begin to categorize the Shadow, you're attempting to resolve it with ego. That won't work – in fact, it just further exacerbates the issues and makes the Shadow even bigger.

The best way to get through this first stage is to become aware of the Shadow and to be aware of any inappropriate or unwarranted emotional outbursts that seem unreasonable relative to their source. At this first stage of recognizing the Shadow, you need to watch for those inappropriate or unwarranted outbursts of anger or fear that are over the top, given whatever prompted them. You scream at your kid for spilling the milk. You get overly anxious when your husband is late from work. You feel like punching out the grocery clerk for throwing the cantaloupe on top of your eggs!

Is it hard in the moment to stop and say, "I'm pretty angry right now. Am I being unreasonable?" Of course it's hard. Right in that moment, you're dealing directly with the Shadow full force.

The first step is to notice it, and if you notice it after the fact rather than during the incident, it's perfectly okay. The important point is that you are beginning to become aware of it. After the fact, you may think, "Wow, that was a little bit out of whack. I flew off the hinge for that?" That awareness begins to bring in the next stage.

A Tip: Shadow issues will show up as:
- Extreme emotional reactions to small events, especially those that happen frequently
- Emotions that seem unconnected to what is occurring
- Dreams that are disturbing
- "Knee jerk" physical or verbal reactions that seem out of context

SECOND PHASE: WE'RE SURROUNDED!

The second phase is, in the cute way my father always put it, "We've been infiltrated!" What does that mean? It means you've seen the enemy and now the enemy is within a close proximity.

It's no longer just out there in the world. It's somehow close now. It's within our family. It's within our business or workplace. It's at church or the dentist. We have been infiltrated by the enemy. It's moving in, circling closer and closer. When you first recognized it, it was distant. Now it's moved in closer and it's not very comfortable when it's close.

A classic example of this is McCarthyism in the 1950's when Senator Joseph McCarthy, a US Senator led the "Red Scare" campaign against communism.

During this time, the US was fighting communism around the world and specifically in Korea. The communist countries seemed aggressive and Americans were genuinely afraid of a potential communist take-over. In early 1950, McCarthy made a speech saying that the communists had already infiltrated not only the country, but our government itself. He claimed to have a specific list of traitors and began a vicious four-year witch hunt to unearth more "enemies of the people" including many members of the State Department, a Secretary of the Army and any Democratic congressmen who had supported Roosevelt's new Deal. (It's interesting to note that McCarthy started his political career as a Democrat himself and supported Roosevelt's New Deal policies in the 1930's. But because he couldn't get elected as a Democrat, McCarthy switched parties.)

McCarthy cast a broad net that included library books (his committee discovered 30,000 books by "communists, pro-communists, former communists, and anti-anti-communists" which libraries were forced to remove from shelves), intellectuals, and those with "sexual perversions" which included homosexuals. (Again, it's interesting to note that evidence later surfaced that McCarthy himself engaged in homosexual activity.)

Eventually, McCarthyism was stopped but not until a lot of good people were labeled as "communists," the scariest Shadow entity of that time for Americans. McCarthy whipped the entire country up into "seeing" communism on every corner.

The first and second stages can overlap. Jung said that the second stage is really where it becomes a mental witch-hunt. In the first stage, you see the Shadow as someone outside. But now it could be anyone – or everyone!

Let's take the example of a health Shadow issue, an imbalance where you're totally rooted in one side. In my world of trainings, an example that I have encountered in the past is that "you've got to be a vegan to be spiritual." Initially, when a person has that issue and they see someone eating a cow, they react, "Ewww!" Enough incidents like that occur and the next logical step is, "You know what? These meat-eating people can be anywhere. I need to seek them out." How many of you have ever done that? A mental witch-hunt where you start noticing *all* the evildoers? All of the meat-eaters, marital cheaters, rude people (or whatever your issue is) seem to show up everywhere. You get a little paranoid. You check with coworkers, "Hey, what kind of food do you eat?"

I had a lady in a weekend training many years ago who, by the very first break, walked up to me and said, "So when are you going to teach the true spirituality?" I said, "What?" She said, "I'm just wondering when you're going to mention, don't eat anything with a face or that came from a face." Her position was as a vegan. Vegan good, not-vegan bad. That's a mental witch hunt. That's where anyone could be a Shadow expression. Anyone and everyone could be the Shadow. It has the feeling of the Shadow moving in.

A person took up a Shadow crusade in Massachusetts. They wanted to institute a law to ban corporal punishment of children and the parents would be jailed if they even spanked their child. In an interview, she said, "It all began very harmlessly with walking through a store." She saw someone spanking a child the day after she had decided no more spanking in her own household. Immediately, I'm thinking, "Shadow. Jung is rolling in his grave." The woman said, "And I saw someone spanking their child and it did nothing because the child kept crying. And she spanked him again and again. And I had to stop her. I did."

Then she continues, "And I realized, maybe my friends spank their children but they just don't do it in public. So I've decided to question my friends, 'Do you spank your children?' And when they said no, I wasn't sure. So I've decided to make this my charge." And oddly enough, she used the term, "I want to slap this law down on everyone." It was amazing watching her. She kept banging the table, slapping the poor innocent table. How did the table feel, man? That piece of wood sitting there crying, "Ow! Ow! Please stop!!!"

How many of you have ever seen that type of thing? How many of you have ever done it, in some area, to a greater or lesser degree? In both of the first two phases, it's important to remember that this is the Shadow moving in. We can get through this phase best by remembering that what we see that we react against is probably a projection of the Shadow, no matter how uncomfortable that feels to say.

THIRD PHASE: IT'S ME!

First, I see my enemy. Second, the witch hunt. "We've been infiltrated. It could be anyone!" The third phase is, "I've seen the enemy and it's me." As you transition to the third stage, you may take on the messages of the third stage consciously: It's actually me. I'm those projections I see." But *the unconscious mind may reject the thinking of the third stage.*

See, in the third stage we face, for the first time, a conflict between our values that we have held dear and that new set of "values" presented by the Shadow. This challenges our present world.

So in the second stage, we're looking for people who aren't what we think we are. "I'm in the light. Are you in the light? If you're not in the light, you're in the dark." "Are you a part of this church? You're not a part of this church? Okay, well, you're evil then." It's that polarizing. "You eat what I eat. Do you believe what I believe?" Cliques in school, cliques in the workplace. But in the stage of "I've seen the enemy and it's me," as Robertson wrote in his book *The Beginner's Guide to Jungian Psychology* is about being ashamed or finding yourself in despair. "Oh, woe is me. The Shadow is everywhere. There's nothing I can do. Everyone is eating cow. And I might succumb to it too!"

We get to this stage by examining the traits in others and realizing that *those same traits lie within us as well.* We know the traits are in us because we project them out. This stage is not about torment even though it can be experienced as torment. This stage is about moving us forward to self-actualization.

Integrating Shadow: Chunking Up
- Notice what is irritating or upsetting you.
- Ask yourself, "What is that an example of?" (bigger picture)
- When you have the answer, you may need to ask again, "And what is this an example of?"
- If the bigger quality is positive, ask yourself, "Where might I be lacking this in my life?"
- If the bigger quality is negative, ask yourself, "How am I reflecting this in my life?"

In NLP, we call this "chunking up" or getting a much bigger perspective on a quality. So, for instance, a student of mine used to get really bent out of shape that "people are so messy." His "enemy" left her dirty dishes in the sink and her shoes all over the place. We had him ask himself, "What is that an example of?" He decided that messiness was a sign of being inconsiderate. What is inconsiderate an example of? In his mind, it was an example of not caring about others or being self-centered. Uh oh. He had to question himself at that point: "Am I uncaring or self-centered?"

Often if you discover the quality that lies one or two logical levels of thinking (the bigger picture) above the Shadow behavior or quality behavior itself, you may find that you arrive to a something that you desperately desire. In the example above, the bigger picture to him was "caring about others" and what he desperately desired was to take care of himself rather than always caring for others. A vegan might suddenly realize that she desperately desires more flexibility in what she eats.

One of my close friends, Kathy Singh said that when she became a vegan (which worked for her), she became a righteous vegan, just like people can become righteous about the Atkins diet or Water Fast Diet or South Beach Diet. "As soon as I became a vegan, I suddenly saw everyone else around me eating meat," she said. "I hadn't noticed it before. I didn't realize how many people ate meat. And I thought I had to take up a cause."

But after a while, she noticed something else: "I realized that they had something that I didn't have. They could go to any restaurant and eat something. They had a flexibility that I so desperately desired, an ability to express themselves." It took her a while, but finally she realized she could have that flexibility too. So you see a behavior in others, not because your unconscious mind wants to torment you – although it can feel like torment at times if you aren't aware that it's part of the process.

Let's use lack of confidence as another example. You see other people as being confident and the less confidence you have, the more confidence you see in others. By the way, you might not initially see "lots of confidence" as a positive thing. Because you lack confidence, you see those other people as being pushy, abrasive or even aggressive.

So you take up a crusade: "I'm not going to allow people to step over others' boundaries." Then you hunt for people around you who are pushy (the witch hunt). But at some point, you might realize that these other people aren't being pushy at all. Maybe you meet someone who allows you to see that it wasn't pushiness, it was congruency and confidence. She actually has self-confidence and she is solid on her foundation - qualities you desperately desire. That's the third stage. You may say, "The enemy is me," but you realize that what you saw as a negative quality is something you actually want for yourself. By noticing what you're noticing or noticing what irks you, then thinking more broadly about it – What is this an example of? – You can discover what it is you want.

A tip for working with the Shadow: When you begin to see the Shadow through these hooks, make note of them. You need to write them down. "Here is a hook. This is something that I see in people that makes me angry. This is something that I look for in people around me." For instance, maybe you track on whether people are smart or not. "Is that guy intelligent? Good. He's one of us. He's in the light. What? He's not intelligent? He's no good then."

At some point, you stop yourself to ask, "Why do I keep looking for that in people?" You look for the hooks: the server who didn't get your order right, the co-worker who sends emails with lots of typos, the person who can't figure out how to get through the security line at the airport. You write them down. You're going to find a pattern, a pattern of what you're looking for in others, a pattern of things that make you angry or fearful. And you've got to take that as a collective and ask yourself, "What is this an example of?" In this case, maybe it's lack of intelligence.

Now if you notice the hooks but then begin to justify your reaction, that's the ego getting in the way. You've got to just write it all down and find the pattern. "This person pissed me off. They smell funny."

Here is an example of justifying the reaction. You react to someone eating meat, and rather than realizing that there is something to learn, you rationalize (with the ego) that eating meat is wrong. Maybe you cite a source that if we allow others to eat meat, we will run out of food, or something similar. You thus ignore the hook that others eating meat has more to do with you, and you miss the opportunity to learn.

By the way, did you know the Dali Lama eats meat? He said so on *Larry King Live*. He has his reasons, and I still find him to be fairly spiritual. I have met amazing spiritual Native Americans and Hawaiians who eat fish and meat. In other words, there are exceptions to this rule. So do you own the issue as being your issue? When you do, you have power to change it. When you blame others, you give away your empowerment. Debbie Ford, best-selling author and renowned expert in the field of emotional education, did a lot of Shadow work in her workshops. She used key words and threw out a whole bunch of key words, like smelly or ugly. If that key word aggravated you, you then would have to explore: What is it that you think is not okay about it? Debbie Ford knew that these key words could activate the Shadow. The key words she used are ones you'd normally reject: "I'm not greedy." "I'm not mean." "I'm not smelly." And your rejection forces the Shadow to show up.

Another way to work with the Shadow is by really taking an honest look at the things that make you angry, the things that make you fearful, the witch hunts that you do. This will allow you to find the pattern. And when you've found the pattern, you simply have to realize that *they* are not the enemy. This is your projection.

FOURTH PHASE: MEA CULPA!

In classic Jungian process, the next phase could be summarized as, "Forgive me, Father, for I have sinned." You have finally become aware that you've been projecting onto other people all this time, beating them up for being such villains in your life. Now you feel bad because you realize it's been *you* all along!

Many people who have done some work on themselves have released a lot of guilt. If so, the fourth phase is pretty easy. The fourth phase is characterized by guilt for how you have behaved or even how you have thought of others. Then you hit remorse: "I shouldn't have been such a bad person, so judgmental, so unkind, so intolerant." We blame ourselves. For example, before we blamed others for lust and we now realize that we were just lusting for something ourselves. So we shift the blame to ourselves.

It's an energetic cycle. "I'm against lusty people." One day, you realize that you were the one being lustful. You mistakenly blamed others, now you go through a phase of blaming yourself. My friend's motto was, "I am only judgmental of judgmental people." And literally one day at lunch, he said to me, "You know, that was judgmental of me, I was really mean." You know you're at this phase in Shadow resolution quite easily: it's when you are experiencing guilt.

Many of us have the tools to deal with this guilt. You've got to forgive yourself. You've got to forgive others. You've got to let go of guilt.

First you successfully get through the third phase, "I've seen the enemy. It's me." Next you enter, "Forgive me, Father, for I have sinned." Here you need to realize that it's not about the lust (or whatever Shadow quality). It's just that you were too rigid and you took such a strong position. You're back to the original creation of the Shadow.

It's important to let go of the negative emotion, to realize that it's just because you took such an extreme position that the Shadow had to naturally project out in such an extreme fashion. You became so rigid in that position that its opposite got pushed out. So in the example of lust: We reject full blown lust but, maybe we could accept self-indulgence. It's okay to indulge yourself every once in a while, right? It's not about lust or absolutely no lust. Indulging the self every once in a while might be a middle ground. Whatever the quality or behavior, remember that the unconscious mind is just attempting to gain balance between opposite viewpoints or opposing viewpoints.

So take my example of the swearing. When I made that decision a while back that I was not going to swear in trainings, suddenly, everyone around me, all my trainers are swearing. I see the enemy. Anyone could be a swearer! I tell those sinful swearers to stop swearing. "No swearing when you go up on stage." I started a mental witch hunt. "No swearing allowed." A couple of them kept swearing. All of a sudden I realized, "I'm the swearer," because I kept yelling at them, "F**k you, guys. Stop swearing!"

I realized, "My goodness, I'm a swearer. I just swore at them. Uh oh,

I've sinned." Then I stopped and it came to me. I felt that moment of freedom when you realize, it's not about swearing or not swearing. If I put charge behind any word and say it in a particular way, it can evoke a response with a group.

There are times to swear and there are times to not swear. It's not about limiting those times or forcing those times. There are some groups that I can swear within more than with other groups. Some groups I do. Some groups I don't. In fact, why do I even bother to think about this consciously?

Swearing is not good or bad. A hundred years ago, shoot and shucks were considered swear words. "Ass" was just a donkey and "bitch" was just a female dog. "Damn" would get you thrown out of places. In a hundred years, f**k, sh*t, and all these other rude words might be normal parts of our vocabulary. You say, "How is that possible?"

There are professors of swearing (yep, it's a professional occupation!) who have mapped it out historically. Studies show that we became numb to those swear words of 50 years ago, and they lose their charge. So people come up with new swear words. Maybe in the future a swear word might be oogy. Google might become a swear word. It's about the charge, not the word.

FIFTH PHASE: IT'S ALL OKAY

So the fifth and final phase of the Shadow resolution is that you just see God in everyone. Everything is valid and has its place. You see that everyone can have their own belief system, their own value system in that area. By integrating the extreme opposite values or extreme opposite beliefs, by reconciling them and integrating them, you are thus integrating the Shadow, absorbing the learnings, and finding that your position has changed.

There can still be a paradox. I can see people out there who have negative or bad intention, but it's no longer a conflict or something that I feel compelled to stop. It's not my job to stop "evildoers." You integrate it and you realize everyone has a different path. Recognizing this and reconciling the Shadow essentially helps you to live 100 percent in the concept of "perception as projection." You can now say, "This is who I am. And it's okay that you are that way or he is that way or she is that way. It's all okay."

For example, I have a diet that works for me, and there are others that eat differently. That is fine, and in fact, I have learned that everybody has a different body. So how can I say that one diet is better than another? I think if one diet worked, we would all be on it.

We can hold that paradox with peace in our hearts. Then we face a new challenge because we wonder how a projection (in retrospect, a *silly* projection) could have become such an extreme issue. Have you ever thought, "I can't believe how big a deal I made about *that*"? If so, you know how it feels to have Shadow resolution.

Now imagine getting to the point where you feel like that with everything. Because once you have resolved one issue, your unconscious mind says, "Okay. Here is the next Shadow issue." Something to look forward to!

INTEGRATING THE SHADOW

Of course, your first step in working with the Shadow is to recognize the Shadow. One good way is to look for emotional outbursts, especially ones that seem all out of proportion to whatever is going on. Also, if a certain person or a certain type of person consistently gets on your nerves, that person is probably acting out a portion or all of the values of your Shadow. So look for emotional outbursts and people that drive you nuts. Let go of the emotion and remind yourself that the person pushing your buttons is just a projection. Your outburst signals a Shadow issue. It just makes things easier to assume that the issue is yours and not some other person's. No matter what comes up, just pretend that it's not their issue. It's all yours. Own it.

And watch for the tendency to throw your "but" in there. "Yes, it's my Shadow *but* that person is really an idiot." "I accept that it's my Shadow issue *but* domestic violence really isn't right." Avoid throwing your but into the situation! (Isn't that a great way to remember it?) That will really help the process move along. And don't cheat by using the word "and." "Yes, it's my Shadow *and* I think people need to stop eating meat." It's your Shadow, period. You've got to practice this at one hundred percent.

You also stay stuck in: "That rapist is my Shadow, but I would never do that." You would be missing the whole point of doing Shadow work. Avoid consciously attempting to wiggle your way out of it. Deal with the emotion. If you're ticked off, let it go. You can't resolve Shadow issues through your ego. If anything, your ego set up the Shadow in the first place by being so rigid in its beliefs.

I've had students tell me, "Dr. Matt, I refuse to do this because then evildoers will become okay." No, they won't. It is definitely not okay with me that people do things like rape. But now, the difference is that I don't have any emotional charge over it anymore. Does that make sense?
If I saw someone beating another person up, I would do everything in my power to stop it and/or prevent it in the first place. You've just got to go back to basic common sense on this one. If you see someone hurting another person, do your best to stop it or get someone else to stop it.

When an action is not appropriate, it *should* give you a charge. It's not appropriate to smack someone around. We teach our kids to avoid doing that. However, after it's done and months have gone by, if you still have a charge on the event, then you have some "stuff" (that's a sophisticated psychological term) that you need to deal with.

Again, resolution of Shadow is not going to negate your sense of right and wrong. All it's going to do is enhance your own ability to be pono[3] with yourself and to know where your boundaries are.

PASSION VS. ANGER

Students have asked, "Well, what about passion? Like passion for a cause or your path?" Good question. The trick is to determine if you're angry about a cause or *passionate* about it. There's a big difference in terms of Shadow work. Have you ever experienced passionate lovemaking? How about angry lovemaking? You should be able to distinguish between anger and passion inside yourself.

Passion feels much different than anger. I still feel passionate about the training I do. But I don't feel like I have to cram it down someone's throat or make them see it the way I do. Another way to look at this is through behavior. A person who says they are passionate about a cause, but shows behaviors of anger, may be covering up issues. There is a clear difference between passion and anger when you look at the behavior.

I have had some students say, "Dr. Matt, these are just labels." Yes, they are, but there are so many examples of those who behave in ways that are clearly passion-based and those that behave out of anger. If you think about it, isn't it pretty easy to spot the difference? You can call it passion all you want. "I'm just passionate about being a vegan!" But that just may be an ego end run to avoid dealing with the Shadow. If you're anything other than flat (meaning, relatively non-charged) about an issue, it's worth investigating.

I think you should be passionate about who *you* are. But I'd be suspicious when you're talking about someone else (unless of course it's the person you're in love with). If you're even hinting that something

---

[3] *I've written a more complete explanation of pono in my book, Foundation of Huna. Basically, it means to feel right with the world and yourself.*

is "their stuff," it's yours. You're still working on the Shadow. Period. Otherwise, you'd be flat on it, and it wouldn't bother you that "this other person" has an issue.

Interestingly, anger and passion are often linked for some. Rejecting anger can dampen authentic passion. But people like artists and actors know that by fully experiencing Shadow emotions of anger or grief, they can more fully tap the passion they need to create and express. By accepting the value of Shadow emotions, you can actually unleash real passion. The trick however is to accept these emotions and to experience these emotions voluntarily – not let them run you!

ABOUT HOOKS

For many of you who have been on a path or done some personal work, the feelings may be a lot more subtle. I know because I've been there. I've been on the path. I know how it feels. You've let go of so much anger and fear that you don't react to the hooks of Shadow issues as dramatically. You don't have huge emotional outbursts. Instead, you sit back and think, "Honestly, these guys really should take responsibility for their action." Are you feeling an irritation or frustration? They are both sub-categories of anger.

At first glance, the books written by Jung or in Jungian Psychology don't seem to really fit for those of us who have been on a path for a while. We've spent a lot of time and energy letting go of anger, sadness, fear and guilt. In *Huna* training, we do this on the very first day. We do it so many times that the hooks are not as evident. The hooks are much more subtle. This is the good news.

You might be reading this thinking, "Damn it. I should have kept my anger so I could spot the Shadow. It would have been easier." Wrong. It's actually easier to deal with the Shadow when the hooks are more subtle and have less of a grip on you. You just have to be more diligent in recognizing those subtler hooks.

For many of us who have done a lot of personal growth and development work, the emotions are present but they are a lot lower in intensity. If I was talking to a group of people who have done no release work, the concept might be easier to grasp and recognize. They could say, "Yeah. You're probably right. I still want to kill that guy." So the hook is obvious.

But many of us don't have those kinds of thoughts. We've studied, meditated, worked forgiveness processes, prayed. Mostly, we're not thrown around by heavy emotion. But it's important to know the difference: Am I relatively unemotional about an issue because I've resolved it? Or am I just avoiding dealing with the Shadow out of laziness because I'm not feeling any great big hairy uncomfortable emotion?

For most people, they know it is the Shadow. If they are angry and/ or emotional that is the Shadow. Well, if you've done a lot of spiritual or personal growth work, you might say, "But I'm not angry and fearful." You've let it go. Anger and fear is gone. But if you're not totally *flat* (unemotional) about it, you want to look at it.

If you have let go of a lot of negative emotions, it will feel more cerebral because it's a belief or a values conflict. If you have sufficiently let go of anger, sadness, fear and guilt, the process is going to feel – listen to my words – *feel* more cerebral. I'm intentionally saying *feel* more cerebral. But it still is feeling.

INTEGRATING THE SHADOW

The first step is to recognize the Shadow and even uncover hooks and triggers so we can integrate the Shadow. As we successfully navigate the Shadow, life becomes more fluid. In fact, you can use that as a barometer to know that you're beginning to integrate the Shadow. It feels like life becomes more fluid, less rigid, less about right and wrong. Values, beliefs are no longer cast in stone - life has more hues and shades of gray beyond the old black and white.

Before the Shadow appears, we regard ourselves as totally separate from the world around us. After, we realize the world is just a haze of projections. When the Shadow is integrated, the world looks brighter.

IS IT EGO OR SHADOW ?

Students have said to me, "I'm not sure if I should be working with the ego or the Shadow?" Simply put, if it's about projections, it's your unconscious (Shadow or other aspects of the unconscious). Your ego is your consciousness. Your ego is not a projection. Having a healthy ego is important. You should have a strong desire to know who you are and what you stand for. That is a part of the path.

Ego is your consciousness. It's who you think you are. The Shadow and the anima and the animus come from the unconscious. They are your not-me projections.

If you are aware that perception is projection, yet you say, "I'm trying to work with my projections, and I can't seem to get it," you may have already integrated your Shadow. You're trying to fix things that are already done. The Shadow is cast by the ego. To understand this, think of your Higher Self as the light (and we will talk more about Higher Self in my next book). The light from your Higher Self shines down on you.

Your ego is that which you believe you are, and the light hitting the ego, casts a Shadow, which is the not-you. It is that which you think you are not.

If you have any projection issue, it's not ego. You can try to fix your ego but how well has that worked for most people? Have you ever just tried to consciously fix your thinking and it works? Some who teach the Law of Attraction promote that approach: "Fix your ego. Just change your thinking." That's conscious mind. But the power to change is really in the unconscious.

Why then did I start this series with a book about the ego and persona? A lot of Jungian psychologists just jump right to the Shadow because that's where the really impactful work is done. But without fully understanding the dynamics of the conscious mind, the persona and the ego, you don't get to a place where you say, "Okay. How do I begin to work with this?"

The Shadow is all that you are not. It's the not-me. It's that which you say, "My ego – I am not this. My ego is this." Therefore, the Shadow is everything you're not. It's what you *think* you're not.

The conscious mind wants to rationalize and think things through. The unconscious mind wants to work it through the emotions. Once we are able to determine consciously (using ego) that which is our Shadow projections and release the emotional baggage attached – the emotional baggage constituting this darkness –we can then more easily incorporate the not-me within our overall consciousness. We have to consciously (using ego) sort through those things that are our projections or Shadow issues.

What is it that's hooking us? What is it that is provoking us? What's pushing our buttons? We need to consciously sort through all of that, then consciously release the emotional baggage housed in the unconscious associated with that issue so that we can more easily incorporate that which is not-me into our overall consciousness.

INTEGRATING THE SHADOW

When the emotional baggage is gone, then the process is about reconciliation of these opposites. There are various processes to do this. One approach is to "reframe" the Shadow aspect you've identified into its positive aspect. For example, say you begin noticing people who have a low flashpoint, who seem to get angry easily and quickly. At the same time, you consider yourself to be someone who is reasonable and rational. Ask yourself the question, "What is the positive aspect of being quick to anger?" Maybe you see that people who are easily angered are more expressive emotionally or maybe that they are more intimately involved in life. When you have identified the positive side of the Shadow aspect, ask yourself, "How might I be missing this positive quality?"

Shadow Integration: Reframing
- Become aware of any negative qualities you are noticing in others that you don't think are part of yourself.
- Make a list of these negative qualities.
- Next, write down the possible positive side of each negative quality.
- Ask yourself, "How or where is this positive aspect lacking in my own life?"

In *Huna*, the technique we use is called the *Keawe* process. I usually teach this to students who have done quite a bit of work to release negative emotions and their baggage through a forgiveness process called *Ho'oponopono*. (See Resources Section to order a free MP3 download of both the Ho'oponopono and the Keawe processes.) In the *Keawe* process, you imagine the personification of the Shadow quality that is not-you. It can be someone you know or just a character that represents it. For example, if the not-you is greedy, you might imagine Ebenezer Scrooge. Next, imagine stepping out of yourself and into that other character to see the world from its eyes. From that perspective, what seemed like greed may feel like caution or building a foundation for the future. Still as that character, ask how this Shadow character perceives you. Ebenezer may see you as careless or unprepared to meet the future. Just notice that different attitude. Finally, you return to yourself and offer those qualities up to Source through Ho'oku'u, calling your higher self. Or, put in a different way, flow love to that Shadow character and thank it for adding balance to your life.

When the baggage is released, the *Keawe* process is very effective in reconciling the opposites, that which is not you.

Shadow Integration: *Keawe* Process
- Imagine a character or person that represents the Shadow quality.
- Step into and become that character.
- Notice how it perceives the world and how it perceives you.
- Return to yourself and offer these Shadow qualities to Source or flow love to that character, thanking it for adding balance to our life.

CONSCIOUS/UNCONSCIOUS INTEGRATION

The ultimate goal is not to deny rationality (conscious) or emotionality (unconscious) but to establish clear communication between the two minds. When working positively, they complement each other in a synergistic way. So deal with the emotions that pop up. Use your conscious mind to pinpoint and find the things you need to let go of, and let the unconscious mind release it.

This is why recognizing the Shadow figure as being a part of your inside is the first process of transcending. One might see it as the first step in transcendence, in self-actualization and individuation, enlightenment, empowerment, whatever word you want to use. We all seek one of those things and integrating the Shadow is a critical part of all of them. Without this integration, what you have denied continues to push you around. Your un-integrated Shadow causes you to *react* emotionally. An integrated Shadow allows you to choose your emotional responses.

BEING FLAT AND BEING EFFECTIVE

When your emotional charge is gone, when there's no hook and when there's no reaction, the issue is not Shadow. When there is a hook, when there is any type of negative emotional response, it's Shadow.

What does it mean to be "completely flat" on something, to have no emotional charge? It doesn't mean that you don't act, that you're sitting back like Switzerland: We're neutral and refuse to take any action either way. (Actually, by doing nothing, you're doing a lot. Philosophically, we could argue that by doing nothing, you're actually still choosing to do something.)

But think of an area where you have no charge. You are flat on it and you're able to go into the situation more clearly. How much better are you at effecting change and transformation? Let's use a work example. Say your team has a decision to make about a project. If you have a preference for one option but realize that the other options would be okay as well, that's a state of being flat about it. You may point out why you think your option is better, but you don't get all riled up about it. And if another option is chosen, you accept it and support it.

How about dealing with your kids? When you're flat on a situation with them, you can actually act like an adult! "Honey, it's okay that you are friends with that person." Or, "Okay, if you think you should get divorced, no problem either way." Rather than getting crazy about how they run their lives, you say things like, "Let's work this through. Let's get this done. How can I help? What do you need to do?"

Sometimes people worry about getting flat or unemotional about situations. "I don't want to get flat on it because that means I'm going to give in. That means I'm going to sacrifice myself, lose my boundaries." That's the ego talking. It's the ego talking when you say, "I'm not going to resolve this because that will mean that they'll be able to run over me." People often avoid resolving the extreme Shadow issues – rape, sexual assault, violence – with the mistaken idea that the acceptance of the Shadow makes those things okay.

But it has nothing to do with that. When you become flat on it, you will still say, "Those things are inappropriate." And you'll be able to respond more effectively, to help someone who has been affected by those things because you're not stuck in an emotional charge.

So what about compassion? Isn't that an emotion? If you feel compassion, are you flat on a situation? That's tricky. According to Webster's dictionary, the definition of compassion implies an emotional charge. Empathy on the other hand is more flat. Empathy merely says, "I feel your pain." But according to the definition, compassion says, "You poor thing! How awful!" I know many of us don't think of compassion that way, but the strict definition implies feeling *compelled* to do something. And that means there's still some Shadow work to be done.

When you're flat on a situation or issue, you're flat on it. Virginia Satir was a highly effective therapist. When she faced clients, for instance in dealing with the husband who beat his wife, her approach was, "Let's assist this guy in getting a new behavior." It definitely wasn't, "Let's fix this son of a bitch!" She was flat, neutral and therefore very successful with her clients.

If compassion to you feels like a positive feeling – "Let's effect some change together. I'm here for you if you need me. If you need some space, totally cool too." – Then you're flat. But if there is any sense of "Poor little you!" and you feel compelled to "fix" them, then it's an indication of Shadow. Honestly, how effective will you be with someone if you view him or her as a victim who needs fixing?

To be really effective in the world, to be powerful in producing change, you've got to be flat on the situation you're facing. That's why this Shadow integration is so important. When you are flat on something, you're unshakeable. You're on your foundation. You have an easier time implementing real change with yourself and others when you are on a solid foundation.

REVIEW OF 5 STAGES

In the first stage of Shadow projection, we're just not really aware of what is happening. It's the typical client coming to a therapy session saying, "My partner has the problem with anger, but as a part of the process, I've just got to come talk to you. But it's my partner who is always angry. Not me." This stage is usually characterized by excessive emotional eruptions, excessive in comparison to their trigger. Your partner gets angry and you fall apart weeping.

There's some charge that is still out of proportion. If there's a charge, then there's something in the Shadow. You've got to celebrate that. It's not about beating yourself up for unresolved issues. It is a cause for celebration because you are becoming consciously aware.
And that's the second stage. This infiltration stage is where you suddenly realize, "Maybe I have some sort of hand in this specific projection that my partner is angry." First stage is: "*He's* angry. Not me."

The second stage is where you think, "Hmmm. I wonder. Is this possibly my projection? I never get angry. How could this be me?" As a second stage, that is a cause for celebration because you are beginning to work with your unconscious mind consciously in integrating the Shadow.

Immediately after recognizing you may have a hand in it, you enter the third stage, which is usually marked by inner conflict. The inner conflict is, "How can this be me?" You start to wake up and become aware. You start seeing angry people everywhere – at work, in traffic, at the mall, on the news. But if you have the inkling that perception is projection, you think, "Wait. What if that's me?" Or maybe you're into the Law of Attraction: "Could I be drawing that to me?" Phase three is, "How can this be me? I'm not an angry person. I love everybody!"

The fourth stage is really a stage of choice. You can either accept the projection as your Shadow, or you can deny it and further repress it. You either accept the projection and admit, "It is me. I've got to figure out what it is" or you work harder to repress it. If you accept the projection, you can figure it out. To you, maybe someone being angry is an example of someone who doesn't love you or who thinks you're unworthy. Once you figure out whatever is underlying your reaction, you then move into the guilty phase: "Wow. That was really dumb that I made such a big deal of it." And once you feel guilty, you know it's time to let go of that guilt.

The final stage is moving to a new level of awareness. "It's okay if people are angry. It doesn't mean they're necessarily angry at me. But if they are, it's okay. They still care about me and I'm still worthy."

THE UNCONSCIOUS BALANCING ACT

The unconscious knows what it's doing. It knows how to create balance. For example, I had a strong belief that what you ate had nothing to do with spirituality. I thought that was pretty reasonable. But I got really rigid in this belief that food has nothing to do with spirituality. So what happens? I kept creating people who would show up in my trainings who adamantly believed food and spirituality were linked up. You see how that works? "Food has nothing to do with spirituality, by gosh." You get rigid on that. So you have people who show up who feel the opposite – strongly feel the opposite! They infiltrated my trainings. They got in my face. I wanted to rewrite our marketing material: "Come to our *Huna* training! Everybody welcome! If you're a vegan, go to hell." I had become the inflexible one.

You can think that your particular belief is so flexible. But then you get rigid in your "flexible" belief: "I'm so flexible. Food has nothing to do with spirituality, period. And it's never going to be any other way." Wham! It pops out to the other side. Your unconscious mind says, "Hmmm. Got to balance this one out." Bingo! Adamant vegans everywhere! But once I got flat on it? Total shift. I still run into lots of vegans but my conflict with vegans has disappeared. The people I meet now seem to have a mutual respect for what others eat. My guess is that they haven't changed, in so much that I have shifted my projections and Shadow issues in this area.

Here's another example of how being in balance and integrating the Shadow can work: At one of our trainings years ago, a new student walked up to the front desk of our hotel on his first night and said, "Where can I get a prostitute?" Oh, my.

My staff had some charge on it. They weren't judgmental about him and his request. They felt protective of our relationship with the hotel. So they had charge from the standpoint of, "Let's get him out now, before he wrecks our reputation! Let him go to another hotel and get as many prostitutes as he wants."

In a sense, it was a healthy, proactive emotion: "Let's get something done." But it was still charged with emotion, not flat. So I said, "No. Let him stay at the training." (I was actually a little curious: Did the hotel provide those services? Could we include that on our welcome packet? I say this in a very sarcastic tone...)

I was flat on it. And what happens? Within a couple of days, on his own, the guy said, "This training is not for me" – and he left. In fact, he had some credit with us for a future training. But he said, "I don't even want a refund. This is such a great training. You guys are a great group. Just take my credit and give all these people some free product."

That's how it works. There was no need for confrontation. Never saw him again. Do you think that that situation could have gone a different way if I hadn't been flat on his request for a prostitute? When you are flat on a situation, you have a greater ability to effect change.

THE SHADOW CYCLE

Once you cycle through the stages and choose to resolve a Shadow issue, what happens next? You get kicked back into the next Shadow issue to deal with and the next Shadow issue to deal with and the next Shadow. So there's a cycling that occurs between those last three stages. You resolve one conflict. It's gone. You resolve it. You see the next one.

If you've done some spiritual or personal growth work and released a lot of negative emotions, the process may go like this. "Okay. Everything is my projection. Rapist, okay. Am I willing to look at it? Yes, I am. Okay. I got it. It was the relationship." Integration done. Okay. I look over there. Aggression. "Aggression, am I willing to look at it? Yes, I am. There's a conflict. Obviously, those values aren't mine. Wait. Let's get a broader perspective. Yes, it is. It's a form of power. It's something I need." Integrate it. See the world in a different way. Next one and next one and next one and next one. The big decision you've made is, "I refuse to play the game of continuing to repress this only to have to deal with it later. I'm going to tackle it right now."

It's a continuous process. You might feel like you're spiraling through the Shadow in the same context over and over and start to question it. "Man, I've already resolved this. I must be doing something wrong." I always like to ask, "Are you spiraling up? Or are you spiraling down? Do you feel that your cycle is moving you up towards higher consciousness? Or are you circling the drain?"

If you're circling the drain, you've got to put on the brakes and start cycling up the other way and expect that it's just a continual process. It may feel like the same Shadow issue but you're probably resolving another facet of that experience. That's okay. You want to make sure you get all the aspects of Shadow.

You can pick your Shadow issues off one by one. But when we get into anima and animus in the next section, you'll see that tackling the big picture issues can have a trickle-down effect where resolving a big one seems to automatically clear a bunch of smaller ones. If you don't know how to tackle the bigger issues, you often spend a lot of time and energy picking off the little Shadow issues one at a time. However, you have to get Shadow toned down sufficiently to begin to really work on the anima and animus because those too are big for some people to go after right away.

APPROACHES TO SHADOW INTEGRATION

As we discussed, to do your Shadow work, you can take various approaches. If you've already experienced a sufficient reduction in emotional charge you can do the Keawe process (see page 46 and Resource Section) or you can use the Shadow integration process on page 45.

But sometimes, you just can't get there because the emotional charge is too strong. In my example of facing the rapist, I just couldn't do the Keawe process immediately and I couldn't find rape's "positive side." It just wasn't comfortable even with all the negative emotions and the limiting decisions I had let go of. So I had to take a little bit more of a cerebral approach that comes from NLP (see page 30). It's the process where you chunk up or take a big picture perspective. You do this by asking what the Shadow aspect is an example of.

For instance, in my case I asked, "Rape, what is that an example of?" I came up with sexual expression. Next I took this broader concept, and asked "So how does sexual expression show up in my life? Is there something out of balance I need to notice?" What I realized was that I felt unexpressed sexually in the relationship I was in at the time. I wasn't able to give or receive the tenderness I needed.

Ninety-something percent of the time, finding this big picture and how it relates to you resolves the Shadow reaction. If it doesn't, you might need to do a little bit more exploration. A student of mine reacted strongly to people spitting in public. So we asked, "What is spitting an example of?" She came up with "crossing or disrespecting someone else's boundaries."

So we asked, "Where in your life are you crossing or disrespecting other people's boundaries?" She was very intuitive with psychic abilities and realized that she didn't always ask permission to use these abilities to find out what was really going on in other people's lives. When she figured out where she was disrespecting boundaries, the next thing to ask herself was, "Am I willing to stop doing that?" If the answer was, "Yes," she could then take action and stop crossing over those boundaries.

When you resolve your real Shadow issue, the one underneath spitting (or whatever it is for you), you don't notice people spitting any more. It seems to disappear and feels like spitting is not in your universe. But resolving it doesn't make spitting okay. A lot of people think, "I don't want to resolve this because I don't think spitting should be okay." It's still inappropriate. It's just that you don't see it anymore. It's not in your experience. There's no charge on it.

If one of your kids started spitting, you would then have no charge. You would just explain, "That's not an appropriate behavior in public. I don't think it's a good idea to just go around spitting. In the state we live in, you don't open up your car door and spit every five seconds. In some states, they do spit. It's like a rite of passage to spit well. But not here."

You get my point? Resolving a Shadow conflict doesn't then make the act okay. It takes a charge off of it. You're no longer experiencing it because you recognized that the Shadow made people spit around you to send you a message that you might be spitting on others in some way, shape or form.

Isn't that amazing how it works? Again, I want to emphasize, resolving and integrating Shadow does not necessarily make that specific behavior okay. It just takes away the charge. Then, when you do see someone spitting, you can approach it in a different, more empowered and less reactive way: "Maybe that person needs a lesson on manners. I don't know." You move on. I believe that sometimes a fear of "if I integrate this, I'll become it" prevents people from dealing with their Shadow, especially in extreme situations.

Dr. Patrick Scott is a student of mine who has a clinic with a few thousand active clients. He has conducted an extensive study on MER (Mental and Emotional Release® Therapy) on clinical depression. Dr. Scott also works with sex offenders, and he was worried that, if he didn't have a charge on that kind of behavior, it would somehow infiltrate him. But by not having a charge, he recognized that he's been more effective in his work. Like Virginia Satir, he could face a sexual offender and say, "The community needs to be protected. It's my job to do it. I need to be flat. There are some sex offenders with whom reform can happen. I'm not dealing with an evil person. It's about the behavior of this person who is in front of me. Let's see if we can effect some change." Isn't it a great place to be? He is just flat with it. But when you are stuck in the emotional charge, it's very difficult to effect change. It's very difficult to assist others in creating change in their lives or even creating change for yourself.

By doing that, Patrick is able to effect greater amounts of change. If you're reading this and thinking, "How can Patrick work in that situation with those kinds of people?" that's really cool because it means you have Shadow work to do on that issue. Patrick doesn't.

THE BLACK BAG

Papa Bray taught a beautiful *Huna* metaphor for one aspect of maintaining a healthy mind-body connection. When individuals had an experience but didn't have the tools to deal with it in the moment, or if they didn't know how or weren't ready to release the emotions connected with it, the unconscious, *unihipili*, took that experience and put it into a metaphorical black bag. The *unihipili* then closed that black bag and stashed it somewhere in the body until the person was equipped or ready to release it.

Take for example the death of a loved one. Emotions that death evokes can be overwhelming to handle initially. Every culture has a different view on the appropriate amount of time for grieving and an appropriate form of expression. If you would not or could not release those emotions appropriately for any reason, *unihipili* stored them into a black bag until the time was right for you. The Hawaiians believed that at some point, either consciously or unconsciously, you would know that it was time to release the experience that had been stuffed into your black bag.

If the realization is conscious, the *Huna* system has a process for internal self therapy or higher self release. As they did in ancient days, you can visit a volcano and symbolically take all of your black bags out and throw them into the volcano to be destroyed, as the late Uncle George Na'ope once described. This would be an example of an external release. The fire element is helpful with transformation and change, so visiting a site that is connected with that element is a form of release. Because "as above, so below" is so powerful, what happens or exists outside, happens and exists inside as well. The external expression (above) affects the internal (below). With guidance from your higher self and some focus, the negative emotion can be released and everything made pono within you again inside, no matter what you are dealing with.

Sometimes, however, your unconscious mind, *unihipili*, decides, "You're ready to let it go." The bag opens and all of the emotions and experiences are relived so they can dissipate. This can happen anytime. We've all experienced having a good day when out of nowhere and for no apparent reason, sadness bubbles up. Papa Bray (who taught my family *Huna*) said this is a signal from *unihipili* that "You're ready to let it go," so it is perfect to express the emotion. In ancient times, if Hawaiians felt sad, they would weep; if they felt anger bubble up, they would express it and allow it to dissipate. As they did so, they knew it was natural and expressed gratitude for the release. They had faith that *unihipili* knew when the time was right and trusted that they had the tools and techniques to handle it. They would release the black bag and move forward.

This points out a difference between Western society and the ancient system of *Huna*. In the West, when negative emotions surface out of nowhere, we panic. We don't see the upheaval as a positive signal from the unconscious that we are ready to resolve the issue, but rather a signal that something is wrong with us. We medicate, we deny, and we avoid. We push those feelings back down below the surface.

To the *Huna* way of thinking, this only confuses the unconscious mind. *Unihipili* is working hard to preserve the body, to release anything that could upset the mind-body balance. The unconscious mind knows that you need to remove the black bag of unreleased negative thoughts and feelings from your neurology before it makes you sick. It can't understand why you won't let that black bag go.

Your unconscious hears you saying, "I want to be happy." So your unconscious mind replies, "Then let go of your sadness." "No," you insist, "I don't want to be sad, I want to be happy." And your unconscious mind repeats, "Okay, then let go of your sadness." You are annoyed now. "There must be something wrong here. I don't want sadness, I want happiness!" Eventually the unconscious mind gives up: "Oy vey. Do what you want!"

In *Huna*, we purposely let go. If a black bag comes up, we are taught to thank our unconscious mind, and honor ourselves by trusting that we have what we need to move through it and let it go. Releasing the black bags is a form of Higher Self release or therapy. The higher self enters the body and the unconscious mind and pulls the black bags out. You don't have to know what's in your bags. It's not our conscious mind's job to remember all the times that you were angry or specifically what made you sad. All the conscious mind has to do is give the higher self permission.

The unconscious mind and the higher self only operate with permission from the conscious mind. A person's conscious mind can deny the existence of the unconscious mind. It can even deny the existence of the higher self. But when permission is granted, the unconscious mind organizes the memories, holds those black bags for you, and signals you when the time for release is right. When you consciously decide that you are ready to release what should be released, the conscious mind invites the higher self in with the help of the *awaiku* (good spirits). All the conscious mind has to do is relax and let it happen, and be willing to let go. The higher self takes care of the rest. The conscious mind's job is to simply allow the other minds or selves to do their jobs. (See Resources to order CD entitled Introduction to Hawaiian Huna to guide you through this process.)

It is not human nature for us to hold on to things because the prime directive of the unconscious mind is to let experiences go. Growing up, you may have been taught that you can't let go of certain issues or emotions quickly. This is your opportunity to change that belief. My mom described my grandfather as a very forgiving person who would let go of any negative emotion as soon as it happened. Have you ever known someone like that? Or known the opposite? The simple question is: Which one do you want to be? It is possible to let go of things easily. It takes an incredible amount of energy to hold onto feelings that are no longer useful for us. What else could you create in your life with the energy that is now dedicated to holding onto what you no longer need?

BLACK BAGS IN THE BODY

With modern technology, these black bags can now be measured. In the book *Foundation Theory*, Dr. Paul Goodwin explains how these black bags can be measured along neuro pathways. He describes how, by using electrical impulses along neural pathways, these repressed emotions show up as blockages along the pathways, and that you can see the change in communication within the nervous system. Many massage therapists run into these black bags as well. While massaging certain problem areas in a client's body, that client might re-experience a wave of old emotions and feel a physical as well as emotional release. The emotions within the black bag had formed a physical blockage or issue. Releasing that physical blockage can help release the emotional black bag as well.

Black bags tend to go where you direct them to go by your language. What do I mean by that? Someone who doesn't like their job and continually says "This job is a pain in the neck" might suffer from difficulty in the neck or head. Any time he or she has a negative experience at work, the unconscious mind puts the black bag exactly where instructed. *Unihipili* likes instructions. It's one of the prime directives. Therefore it's important to be aware of your language. If you habitually use phrases like, "I have a heavy heart because of that situation," enough black bags will accumulate in that area to create a profound physiological affect.

Comments that connect emotions with body symptoms are either giving the unconscious mind instructions, or they're expressing how someone experiences the black bags. Psychological studies have shown that certain emotions have more impact on the heart, for example. Many articles published in the *Journal of the American Medical Association* relate anger to heart-related issues. The entire focus of the discipline in psychology called PNI (psychoneuroimmunology) focuses on studying how specific stressors affect specific areas of the body. Dr. Deepak Chopra is one of the founders of PNI and is credited with early research in this area. This is key: If you never tell the black bags where to go, *unihipili* will spread them out rather than letting them pile up in one area.

Another important question is whether negative emotions are bad. I don't believe they are. Negative emotions like anger, sadness, fear and guilt provide us with feedback about our surroundings and our experiences. If every time you walk into a certain location, you feel fear, that's a clue! Don't go there!

What *Huna* proposes is that holding on to the negative emotions past the point where they are ready for a natural release is unhealthy for the mind, body and spirit. That release is our focus when we do *ho'oku'u* or higher self therapy. (See Resources to order CD for this process.)

DOES THE THIEF WANT TO GET CAUGHT?

I think it's inaccurate when people say, "The thief wants to get caught." I don't think the unconscious mind increases the Shadow emotions or behavior to make sure you "get caught." It does it to catch your conscious attention and bring you back to balance. I once took a criminal profiling course from Marx Howell. His opinion wasn't actually that these people wanted to get caught. His opinion, through psychological research, is that the thrill of whatever they're doing is not enough, so they just up the ante. By the very nature of increasing the behavior, they're going to get caught. It's inevitable. If you like blowing things up, eventually you'll blow something big enough up that someone else will see.

I don't know if the over-eater wants to get caught. If it's truly a cry for help, or if it's just getting farther and farther and farther out of balance. The swings become more noticeable and by the very nature of the swing of that cycle and rhythm that teeter-totter gets bigger. The two ends are going to be more visible from a greater distance. I don't think that the politicians whose jobs depend on maintaining their persona actually want to get caught or that religious leaders want to be exposed doing things that they know to be "sinful."

But it's quite possible that the unconscious pushes them to the limit of behavior, exposes their Shadow issues in obvious ways, so that they are forced to move to balance. It isn't a conscious "wanting to get caught," but an unconscious desire to move to balance.

EGO INTERFERENCE WITH THE UNCONSCIOUS

On the process of individuation, we need to be a totally trustworthy parental spirit to our unconscious mind. We have to be Dr. Patrick Scott to the sex offenders in our approach to dealing with our Shadow issues. To become judgmental about our projections slows down the process of evolution. If you cop the attitude of "I can't believe I'm irritated by spitters," you are telling your unconscious mind, "I don't believe you're actually trying to help me to resolve a Shadow issue imbalance." And that's the voice of our ego.

Our ego will slow down the process of self-actualization. Some people, when they think they've got it all figured out, prematurely close or stop the process. That's the ego talking. Or "I can't believe I have to go through this again. What? Again?" Ego again. When the ego is a totally trustworthy parent to the unconscious, it says, "Great. We must be taking it to another level." This is the ego showing respect for the unconscious.

Remember how flat Dr. Scott was in working with one of the most hated populations within the prison system? That is the attitude we need to practice with ourselves. It's how the higher self views us, with total non-judgment. When the Shadow pops up again, you don't want to judge it as "bad." You don't want to close the door because you think you've achieved a certain level so you are "beyond all that." Instead, you want to accept it as the unconscious mind taking you to the next level.

When you're working with the Shadow, there is that tendency to get a lot done and then slip back into the ego. You see this with "self-help gurus." They do a sufficient amount of work with the Shadow then think, "I know enough now." Their ego actually kicks up a notch. They decide to begin teaching, rather than waiting until they have self-actualized and connected with higher consciousness and the flow that comes from it. They've peeled a couple layers of the onion back, and think, "Hot dog! I've got it!"

This can happen anywhere to anyone. In a relationship: "Man, I've hit jackpot nirvana, met the right person. Don't have to do anything else." Really? How many years do you plan to be with this person? That's like saying, "I ate that salad today. I'm all done. I am totally healthy forever."

I think this is why people mistakenly say, "Let's eradicate the ego." We don't need to eradicate the ego. But we do need to connect fully with Self. And I believe that you do need to consciously practice having a healthy ego. All the while realizing that, as you always will have an ego, you're going to continue to cast a Shadow.

PROGRESSION OF THE PROCESS

As you begin to resolve the Shadow, you'll notice a shift in your awareness of your reactions. First, you notice a charged reaction after the fact, after you've calmed down. "Wow, I really blew up. I feel bad for that door!" Next, you begin to notice your reaction on the tail end. As you're blowing up and coming off the emotion, you think, "Wow, that was an unnecessary response." As you continue the process, you notice it in the moment, almost like an observer where you're saying to yourself, "I can't believe I'm blowing up" even as you continue to blow up. In the next stage, you get it to a point where you say, "I can feel that I'm about to blow up." In that moment, you know that you have a choice about whether to go with the reaction or not.

You still, by the way, the first few times, may blow up just for the grin. It's a process. But after a while, you feel the reactive emotions coming up. You feel your hands clenching. And you say, "Wait a minute. I've done this game before. I know how it's going to end. I've acted this way before. Wait, wait, wait." Then you can celebrate because you didn't have that angry or fearful explosion. You might feel guilty that you even had a whiff of a reaction – and of course, you need to release that guilt. And eventually, you never even get to the point where you have the thought.

If you're able to slow it down to the point where you're able to recognize the dichotomy, then the idea may be to do the Keawe process (see page 46) right there because you have the ability to resolve that dichotomy. You might as well take advantage of being associated in the moment to the opposites.

During this process, your ego still has a job to do. It can't resolve the Shadow but it decides to allow the process – or avoid it. The unconscious can't resolve it without the ego's cooperation. It's like *Ho'oponopono*, the forgiveness process used in *Huna* to help release emotional baggage (see Resources to order free MP3 download). I've heard students say, "I just ask my unconscious mind to do it. I don't need to do it consciously."

Really? If you've done Ho'oponopono as many times as I have, you can do it in five minutes. Really get the kinesthetic knowing that real forgiveness has happened. It only takes five minutes but I have to consciously choose to do it. I don't just tell my unconscious mind, "Every night at around 6PM, you just do it while I'm popping popcorn and watching football." That's disrespectful. That's the ego telling the unconscious mind to just do its job. That would be like a conductor telling the orchestra, "Just play Beethoven's Ninth. Do I really have to be there and wave the silly little stick?" It would be like the boss just walking by and saying, "You guys just do your job. Okay. I'm going to go sit on the beach."

The unconscious mind is in charge of so much work to do: digest your food, beat your heart, breathe you. Can you expect it to, "Oh by the way, just do some *Ho'oponopono* while I watch Will and Grace."

No. You need to have a healthy ego. A healthy ego doesn't say, "I've done enough work that I can just tell my unconscious mind to do it from now on." You're still the conductor. You've got to be there. You've got to be present.

ANIMA ANIMUS

If the Shadow is that which we despise, the anima animus is that which we desire. The anima is the personification of all of the feminine psychological tendencies within a man. They are the archetypal feminine symbolism within the man's unconscious.

The animus is the personification of all masculine psychological tendencies within a woman. In other words, they are the archetypal masculine symbolism within a woman's unconscious mind. A man has an anima and a woman has an animus. In Latin, these words mean "soul."

The first thing that I want to do is make sure that we get our brains wrapped around the label. Most books say that Jung picked anima / animus because Latin made the concepts sound more scientific. Books that take a more esoteric or spiritual approach to Jung's work view anima / animus as the yin - yang symbol. The idea is that you are on one side as a physical and energetic male or female, and you carry inside you that small yin / yang symbol of both.

You project out onto the other side, then, the opposite of you. So if you are a man, you have anima, the feminine external projection. For women, the external masculine projection is animus.

Jung once said, "You marry your unconscious mind and project all of your unresolved material onto her." We're getting into that concept now because once you've dealt with Shadow, you are left to face your partner.

Jung and Jungian psychologists would start with the sex that you are born and assume that your initial projection will be that of the opposite sex. Once you begin to do any anima-animus work, you need to see which one it is that you personally need to integrate or resolve.

The anima and animus get their influence from the collective unconscious which is closer to higher self than the Shadow. According to Jungian perspective anima and animus are in the realm of the collective, outside of the personal unconscious. The Shadow is very personal to you and resides in the personal unconscious. But though characteristics of the anima or the animus come from the collective, they are also influenced by a person's individual experience.

The anima and the animus derive their influence from the collective but also from an individual's personal experience growing up. What is the ideal woman for a man? What is the ideal for a specific man? One of the first encounters of the anima-animus is with the mother-father archetype. For the majority of children growing up, father-mother is their first experience of the male-female archetypes, which is why Jung, in a very drastically different way than Freud and Adler did, still focused attention on mother and father, but as personifications of anima and animus. This is why children have a particularly special bond with the opposite sex.

Have you ever met a man who is still a mama's boy? He has not yet transitioned his anima off his mom. An adult woman who is still daddy's little girl has not yet transitioned her animus off of the father.

Anima and animus have three characteristics.
1) A natural, unconscious tendency for appearing as the opposite sex in our projections. In other words, the masculine or feminine archetype.

2) They can emerge as descriptions and symbols of femininity or masculinity passed down through myth, art, fairy tales and religion, which are all profoundly influenced by the archetypes.

The archetypical woman and man in art, painting, story, and myth change over time. The archetypical anima and animus were drastically different 100 years ago, 200 years ago, 500 years ago, 2,000 years ago. These things are not fixed. They are types of energy that are commonly agreed upon within a time and culture.

Have you watched any cartoons of superheroes recently? Let's take Batman for example: Bruce Wayne started as a skinny stick in tights. Now even when they put George Clooney in his Batman suit, his shoulders are bigger than a door frame. In the cartoons they're even bigger! The original G.I. Joe was just a normal guy. Now even the action figures are so huge as to look like they have ingested three doses of steroids for breakfast. Tinker Bell's dress is definitely shorter.

3) The third characteristic of anima and animus is that they emerge as personal experiences of the opposite sex.

The anima and the animus can sometimes take on a god-like or goddess-like experience. When two people first come together, even a rubbish boyfriend looks like the animus. As the relationship continues, based on a lack of resolution of things like the Shadow, we begin to peel away or chip away at the outer layer. We find that this person does not live up to our anima or animus. So we begin to seek it elsewhere in another partner. "Why can't you be more like him? Why can't you be like Batman?" "Because I'm not," he says. "Well, you should be." All you're saying is you're not living up to my animus, dude.

Actually, it's not another person's job to live up to your anima or animus. Oddly enough, the person doesn't measure up may be perfect for you.

When you have an imbalance in the anima-animus, the person can never be who they truly are to you because you see them through such an amazingly wonderful filter of unrealistic expectation. But it doesn't matter because you won't find true balance in the exterior. You have to bring balance inside yourself because where did the anima or animus come from? You.

The key with the anima and the animus is not just how you deal with the external projection. It does affect all of your relationships and especially your relationship with the other aspect of creation. But it's also about how you reconcile it within yourself as well.

I grew up in Hawai'i and have a very close connection with things like hula and chanting. When I began hula, I was still slightly uncomfortable that it was too feminine, especially for a non-native Hawaiian. Chanting was okay –but odds are that if you were into chanting, you were into hula. I wasn't so uncomfortable with chanting and hula that I wanted to stop, but I kept it pretty private.

Most people, including my mom never heard me chant until my wedding day. One of my mentors, Uncle George Na'ope, was there. He stood up and chanted. I sat there, my ego aglow. "This is so cool. Look at this. My mom is here. Uncle is here chanting at my wedding."

When he finished chanting, and he pointed to another of my teachers, Kumu Hula Etua Lopes. "Chant." I thought, "Hmmm. Wait a minute." Etua stood up and chanted. Etua finished and Uncle pointed to my father. "Chant." At that point, while my father is chanting, I felt a bead of sweat dripping down my back. I knew what was coming. Did you ever wish time would slow down or stop completely, but it just doesn't?

My dad finished chanting. The whole room is stunned at this point. There are friends and relatives who have never, ever seen my dad, let alone a white guy get up and chant. Uncle George turned to me and said, "Chant." Well, when Uncle says chant, it's very Pavlovian. Ding, ding, ding.

I stood up and the chant *Noho ana ke akua* came right out. Though I was able to chant, I was still self-conscious. "Now everyone knows I chant and probably guesses I do hula." In that discomfort, I was sure that my mom's expression said, "Oh my God, what's coming out of his voice? Should I give him a Heimlich or something?"

It took me many years before I actually felt comfortable getting up and dancing hula in my workshops. The reason was that I was still working on integrating my anima to allow myself to be okay with feminine and a masculine. As my Kuma Hula (teacher of Hula) Etua says, "Each of us carries both inside." Are they in balance? Or are you projecting all of it out onto your partner? You see, balancing the anima and animus is balancing the feminine and masculine within. Dancing hula is seen as feminine and if you think "only women do that" you could be denying the aspect inside you.

To balance feminine/masculine inside you, to balance yourself with the other half of creation, is an important step on the path to actualization. In the realm of dichotomies, anima and animus are especially important because they allow you to reconcile the opposite energies that represent all of creation: the active and the passive principle, yin and yang. At the very highest level, all energies are one. According to *Huna* and to Jung, the very first and biggest division into separate energies is the female/male, yin/yang, passive/active dichotomy. In Hawaiian it was *Kane* and *Na Wahine*.

You can work on the smaller dichotomies in your life. But if you can process this big one, it resolves a lot. However, you cannot fully appreciate or get to this work if you are still struggling with major Shadow issues. I began to work on anima-animus while I still was working on Shadow issues. I do believe you can work on both, but when you really integrate the Shadow aspects, the next thing that pops up is anima-animus. The anima-animus issue usually feels like an overall imbalance of energy at a very deep level. That said, the work is not really a linear process: "I integrate Shadow then balance anima-animus and – BAM! – I'm done!" No, actually you'll find that it happens in cycles.

ANIMA PROJECTION

The undiscriminating man associates with those personal qualities that are symbolically masculine. He expands these aptitudes and to some extent integrates their unconscious influences into his conscious mind's personality. By "undiscriminating," I mean a man who is not really aware, not particularly introspective. This is the type of guy who doesn't question much, who may not be very interested in personal or spiritual growth.

This undiscriminating man expands the aptitudes that are symbolically masculine and integrates their unconscious influences into his conscious mind's personality. What does that mean? The unconscious, undiscriminating guy basically takes everything that we stereotype as masculine and makes that his personality: "I've got to be tough. I don't cry. I don't hug my kids. When I come home, it's my way or the highway. Dinner better be on the table." The masculine stereotype or archetype is different in different eras. Maybe today's archetypal man doesn't have to be the sole breadwinner though he still might expect the female in his life to nurture the kids and get dinner on the table. The undiscriminating male will totally buy into whatever the masculine archetype of his era is – or even choose one from the past.

It's the undiscriminating man, the man who isn't interested in questioning the role he plays, who says, "What do you expect? I'm a man." He can't admit to possessing qualities that are feminine. "No, I don't cry. I'm not gonna hug the kids. You fell down? Go talk to your mom."

He does not admit to possess the qualities that are symbolically female or feminine as a part of his own personality. Rather, he projects them onto women.

The undiscriminating man embodies what we archetypically experience as the man, denies having any feminine, and projects the feminine onto women around him. He will even perceive an empowered woman as his projection of the anima. If in his mind the anima is helpless and emotional, he'll still manage to view even a powerful woman as needy and moody. He is projecting his anima – those distinctive, feminine potentialities that are significant components of his unconscious mind.

This is an important point to grasp: The undiscriminating man will project his anima (those particular, distinctive, feminine potentialities that are significant components of his unconscious mind) onto women around him. And, because the characteristics of his anima are significant to him, they carry a *significant emotional charge*.

And please pay careful attention to this: He will project his anima (those distinctive, feminine potentialities that are significant components of his unconscious mind which therefore carry an emotional charge) onto a few women for whom he will feel strong and compelling emotion, usually positive, but occasionally negative. Obsession and fascination manifesting as an instant, powerful attraction for a woman about whom he knows little or nothing is one of the signs of the anima projection.

We've all had that experience, right? You're watching TV or watching a movie. You see a movie star (who, by the way, is pretending to be someone else) and for a brief moment you think, "She's really my type! I'd love to meet her." Consciously, you know she's not who she appears to be. She may even be some prima donna cocaine addict playing the role of the Virgin Mary! But even though you know that, you still feel this urge, this strong hook, and get caught up in the fantasy. Music plays and all rational thinking disappears. Then your girlfriend sees the look and slaps you back to your senses! (Or did that only happen to me??) It doesn't matter that you're "spiritually evolved." It still happens! And of course, it happens for women as well who, by the way, are more apt to admit it. Why don't men admit it readily? Because the undiscriminating man associates with the personality that are archetypically male, he would never admit to disloyalty or childish fantasy –"No, honey. I love you. I only have eyes for you." – because that's the archetypical guy.

A hint: You know you have anima work to do if you still find that obsessive fascination hook when someone simply walks by. You just see that person and are ready to worship at her altar! It's an urge that is beyond just recognizing beauty in another person. In fact, it is liberating to get to a point where you are able to recognize beauty in other people and yet have your anima firmly attached to the person you are in a committed relationship with. But obsession or fascination manifesting as an instant, powerful attraction for a woman about whom a man knows little or nothing is one of the signs of an anima projection.

The undiscriminating man has not consciously developed any of his feminine qualities. A couple of the universal feminine qualities that both Jung and Papa Bray talked about were strong expression of emotions and need for committed relationship. Today, men are supposed to be able to express their emotions but most of us are still stuck with the role models of John Wayne or Dirty Harry. The masculine hero in movies still keeps his emotions in check as he bashes the bad guys. The sweet, emotional Mr. Mom character tends to show up only in comedies, not as a role model to follow.

The undiscriminating man doesn't feel that he needs to commit to a relationship. I've heard men say, "Well, it's in our DNA, you know? Because in ancient times, we had to procreate. So men needed lots of women." I heard a guy say once, "You've got to spread the seed, man. You've got to plant your seed, and the field's big." (Please forgive my being direct; I am just saying what I heard!!!)

So since the undiscriminating man has not consciously developed any of his feminine qualities, the anima aspect of his personality is suitable for being ensnared or possessed. When whatever qualities a man is suppressing and denying come along, it's really easy for the guy to fall under the spell. Remember *Bewitched*, the old TV show? Growing up, I took the anima off of my mom and put it right on to Elizabeth Montgomery. I wanted to name my kid Tabitha or Samantha or something!

But just imagine that a woman can wiggle her nose and the man acts out emotional behaviors and relationships in irresponsible, foolish, and immature ways that are apparent to others but not to him. This is pretty much how it works. A man gets hooked by his anima, all the qualities that he's denying and a woman who has those qualities comes along. He becomes bewitched. He acts like an idiot. Here are the key words to remember: *irresponsible, foolish, and immature.* Your friends look at the way you act around her and say, "Dude, you're crazy. You shouldn't be giving her all your money." But you can't hear them: "No, I'm not crazy. I'm in love!" When the anima hook occurs, the unconscious man will act irresponsible, foolish, and immature – *and* be in total denial of it, *and* love it!

Now it's a different story when the undiscriminating man sees the feminine qualities he unconsciously desires in another man. In that case, the man displaying feminine qualities becomes the enemy. This is why in our recent history there's been so much persecution against gay men because men see in them that quality of wanting to be feminine and they just want to just squash that. And it's not just about being gay. There's a reaction to any man who cries, Mark McGwire for instance. I remember when he retired and cried. I was with a bunch of other men who said, "Oh, that's it. I just lost all respect. If I was in the room, I'd punch him." All because Mark McGwire, the Home Run King, became emotional and showed an archetypical feminine quality.

But that example would not be classified as an anima/animus issue. That's a Shadow projection because it's the man seeing something in a man. When the projection or reaction is with the same sex (a man projecting to another man, a woman projecting on to another woman), it is the Shadow. When the projection is on to someone of the opposite sex, it is an anima/animus issue.

ANIMUS PROJECTION

The animus projection is pretty much the same as the anima projection but the reverse. Women have an animus. The undiscriminating woman associates with those personality qualities that are symbolically feminine just as the undiscriminating man associates with personality qualities that are symbolically masculine. She expands these aptitudes to some extent and integrates their unconscious influences into her conscious mind's personality.

What does that mean? It means a woman grows up learning what a woman is supposed to be and says, "I'm going to take this on as my ego, my persona. I will take on that persona as I am supposed to." She consciously identifies with the feminine. On the other hand, she does not admit to possess qualities that are symbolically masculine as a part of her own personality but rather projects those qualities onto men. So consciously she identifies with women. Unconsciously, she projects the masculine onto men.

She will project her animus – those particular distinctive masculine potentialities that are significant components of her unconscious mind and therefore carry a special emotional charge – onto a few men for whom she will then feel a strong compelling emotion, usually positive but occasionally negative. This is exactly the same dynamic as with the anima in men. And like men, obsession and fascination manifesting as an instant powerful attraction for a man about whom she knows little or nothing is one of those signs of an animus projection.

In a recent workshop on this, a female student asked, "Why would a woman go out to nightclubs time and time again and hook up with guys that she's never met?" I would say there are two things going on in that example. One is that everyone has a slightly different projection of their anima and animus. Everyone has a different hook. For example, blondes just aren't my type. When Soomi dyes her hair black and goes to her natural color, I actually like that better. So you can't say all men prefer blondes. My mom made that joke once and then turned to my wife Soomi and said, "Oops, sorry, honey." Soomi responded, "I don't care. He'll like whatever color I put up there." So the first thing to understand is that every man and woman has a slightly different hook. So the woman who is bar hopping may have a thing for guys who drink or guys who party or guys who don't want to commit – who knows?

However, if the hook remains unresolved and you have not yet owned it and internalized it, then it can become an obsession and fascination. You find yourself constantly seeking it out there, jumping from man to man or woman to woman because that emotional charge becomes the thrill.

The other thing to notice about this example is that the woman asking the question had some unresolved issues because "women going to bars" had such a charge for her. In this case, because her attitude was "I would never do this!" the issue was a Shadow issue, not an anima-animus imbalance.

How many women watching *Iron Man* would say, "I would so marry Robert Downey, Jr.!" He is a terrific actor, but off-camera, he apparently was a heroin addict. Do these women really want to marry a heroin addict (or former heroin addict)? No! They are lusting after Tony Stark, the guy with the great cars and the Iron Man suit who rescues damsels in distress on the way to saving with the rest of the world. If you're right there in the middle of the movie and even for a brief moment that obsession or fascination kicks in, that's the animus.

I wasn't a big *Friends* fan, but I happened to catch an episode where each character was allowed to make a list of five people that you'd be allowed to cheat on your spouse with. What was that saying? It said: "Let's celebrate our unresolved anima and animus. If a person contains that particularly strong hook for you, go for it!"

The undiscriminating woman has not consciously developed any of her masculine qualities. Jung listed these qualities as: logic, leadership, and need for independence. But is this still true in our post-women's lib culture? Think about it: How often is a strong woman characterized as pushy, uppity or any number of not-so-polite words?

Even now, men are not supposed to be emotional. They're not supposed to want a relationship. They're supposed to be independent, logical. Women, on the other hand are supposed to be needy. They're supposed to want a relationship, be vulnerable, illogical, irrational.

My wife, Soomi, along with a few of the women who work in my organization, has been characterized as pushy. I've had one or two people in the weekend trainings over the past decade come up to me and say, "I can't believe you married her. She is one pushy so and so." By the way, see, when a woman who is undiscriminating and unconscious and has not yet developed her animus and integrated it reacts to another woman who has integrated these qualities, that's a Shadow reaction because it's same sex. She sees in the other woman what she unconsciously desires, so that other woman becomes the enemy.

My wife (like my mom and other women I work with) is so empowered that she can stand in her own light and push back on things she doesn't care for. Is that pushy? Or, is that empowered? The answer is yes and no. It depends on how you perceive it

Remember when a man is ensnared by the anima, he acts out emotional behaviors and relationships by being irresponsible, foolish, immature. But according to Jung, when women are ensnared by the animus, they act out by behaviors and emotions of opinionated, argumentative, domineering. When women are ensnared it activates those opposite qualities inside of them. They act out of those qualities that have been suppressed but in negative ways. So independence and leadership become argumentative and domineering. A man when ensnared by his anima becomes the negative of emotional and committed to relationship. He acts out as irrational and needy. Two weeks before meeting the woman who hooks his anima, he insists that men don't cry. After meeting her, he's a weepy, whiney mess. A woman who believes she is supposed to be caring and loving, not pushy, will become the negative qualities of leadership and logical and become totally pushy, aggressive, domineering after being ensnared and possessed by her animus.

Of course, she will deny this. The femme fatale: What's the classic movie example of the femme fatale? *Fatal Attraction*, a woman ensnared by then spurned by her animus. She gets a little pushy, then aggressive, then shows up in his house and boils the bunny!

A woman who is ensnared by her animus becomes a stalker, but in a uniquely different way than a man ensnared by his anima. Her stalking response is aggressive, pointed. His stalking response tends to be more emotional and irrational. The man becomes those feminine qualities to the negative and extreme. The woman who has denied her masculine becomes those same masculine qualities to a negative and extreme. She becomes the *Wayne's World* psycho hosebeast. You turn the corner and she's there.

This is classic Jung. A key to this is that the man or woman when possessed or ensnared by their anima or animus does not – absolutely, without a doubt does not – believe that they are acting out of character. "No, there's nothing wrong with me sitting outside of his house for the entire day, damn it. I just had to make sure." Jung pointed out that the man or woman will vehemently deny they are acting out in inappropriate ways: "What are you talking about? I love her, damn it. I'm doing it for her own good." But when you are accused of acting out, that probably is your projection pointing out something you need to investigate. In other words, if a friend accuses you of being an idiot, you probably want to pay attention!

What I'm describing is the negative pointer. When the undiscriminating, unconscious man and woman gets that hook into the anima or animus, when they feel as if they've become possessed, the qualities that have been pushed down come to the surface. These qualities surface because of our whole naturally regulating system of balance but they surface in an unhealthy way.

It's not always that the anima or animus has rejected someone. Once you are ensnared, those qualities can come up with or without rejection, even without the perception of rejection. A man when ensnared by his anima in the beginning of the relationship will act in those ways to some extent. A woman ensnared by her animus in the beginning of a relationship will act in those ways to some extent. It's not uncommon for a woman to start dating someone and claim, "Oh, I'm totally flexible. No worries. Anything goes." Then a month later, she's screaming, "If you even get in the same zip code as your ex, we're done!" Or what about the guy who seems so calm and cool when you begin the relationship? After a few dates, he's on the phone crying because you want to hang out with your friends on a Saturday night. It has nothing to do with rejection. However, a rejection definitely triggers it. If you are hooked and that person then rejects you, it definitely can intensify the reaction.

As a woman, if you see another woman getting hooked by her animus and think, "What an idiot!" that's actually your own Shadow issues. More often than not, Shadow is same sex and anima/animus is opposite sex. Is it possible for the reverse to be true? Of course it is. In any given situation, anything else is possible. However, the typical response is Shadow if it's same.

As someone who sees that a friend is being hooked by their anima/animus, there's hardly anything you can do except deal with it internally. Just realize it's a part of your friend's path. At some point the halo falls off and the shining armor begins to rust. If you are a close enough friend, your buddy might come to you and ask, "What do you think I should do?" It's only at that point that you'll be able to offer some insight.

Because when they're hooked, they're like a fish with the hook in its jaw. They're busy struggling and fighting for pure survival. If you resolve the issue within yourself, you're flat on it. So when your friend comes to ask you for advice, you can be helpful. If you still have a charge on it ("You idiot, what are you doing?!?"), there's nothing you can do. If anything, you'll just exacerbate the situation.

Years ago, I had a friend who was totally hooked on a woman. I kept quiet and worked my own internal process until I was flat on it. Finally this friend noticed that his shiny new perfect partner really wasn't so perfect. He came to me and asked, "What should I do?" Because I was flat on it, I was able to say, "Here's what you should do. You should stick it out. Because you might actually get some learning from this situation. Because you've gotten past this hump and, of course, no one is perfect." I think it really helped him out, but only because I was flat on it. If I'd still had any charge on the situation, I wouldn't have done that. I would have told him to run for the hills! Because when you are unresolved about a situation, actually another person's issue can be bigger for you than for the person in the situation.

ANIMA/ANIMUS INTEGRATION

The integration of the anima and animus closely resembles the ancient concept of the *mahu*. The word *mahu* is used as slang today and has many meanings. But in ancient culture, *mahu* meant a person who had a complete integration of anima or animus. In some Polynesian cultures in the Pacific, Uncle George explained that if five boys were born in a family, the fifth one was raised mahu or feminine because the family needed feminine energy in the house. Even while doing this, they didn't forget that individual was still a boy. They didn't strip the man, even if he was feminine, of his masculinity.

In ancient times, the *mahu* was prized in Hawai'i according to Uncle George because the individual had the ability to switch to either side of the male/female dichotomy without any conflict. And that ability was considered to be enlightened. The true kahuna (a master or expert in a particular knowledge) has the ability to hold two conflicting values, two conflicting beliefs without experiencing conflict in the mind. So the *mahu* were prized as being very spiritually evolved because they had reconciled the anima and the animus sufficiently that within themselves they were both masculine and feminine. They were self-sufficient beings.

But what about today? For someone who is gay or lesbian in today's world, this integration doesn't necessarily happen. In our culture right now with the pressure, the stereotypes, and the archetypes put on gay, lesbian, transgendered, bisexual, do you think they have lots to work through Shadow-wise? When I've discussed this with friends who are gay or lesbian, they say, "Definitely!" Though 200 years ago, several cultures celebrated genderless or gender-crossing people, that just isn't so today. These perspectives are passed down ethnically, culturally, and religiously. We're told, "Here's what's right; here's what's wrong." If we grow up with cartoons that say this is the way a woman or man should look and act, that image gets ingrained. It comes out of the collective.

By the way, if you are heterosexual, you won't become gay or lesbian by resolving anima/animus issues. But integration of anima in heterosexual men will make them feel comfortable getting up and dancing a hula that is very feminine without a feeling worrying that their masculinity will come into question. In fact, before I did this type of integration work, I would worry that people seeing me dance, might think I was too feminine. But today, because I do the hula so often, I probably wear a skirt more often than my wife Soomi. I resolved it, and actually I have had students (men and women) say, "Wow, it must be great you know how to move your hips so well!"

It allows a man to own the feminine aspect inside himself. Integration of the animus in a female might allow that woman to feel comfortable in competitive arenas such as sports or business. It doesn't negate her feminine side. This is one of the keys to recognizing integration: It doesn't do anything other than allow you to be comfortable with who you are, both the masculine and the feminine.

Integration of the anima/animus in partners allows them to be able to switch the polarity sufficiently within the relationship. Even in a same sex relationship, there needs to be a physical polarity where one is the feminine and the other is the masculine. In relationships, both same sex and heterosexual, this polarity may be fixed or it may shift back and forth depending on the time or circumstance. In relationships where it is easy for that polarity to shift, there's not as strong a barrier between the anima and animus and the partners are typically more balanced within themselves.

When one is on good terms with their anima and animus, he or she can be a valuable messenger between the unconscious and the conscious. So one of the reasons you want to work on resolving the anima and animus is that it opens up the connection and the communication between you and your unconscious. Another benefit of integration is that you can avoid being taken over by the anima/animus and control these projections by integrating the opposite sex archetype into consciousness. It also opens up your potential.

We restrict our experience to only half of our potential by only identifying with those qualities that match our sex. That's worth repeating: We are only at half our potential if we limit ourselves by identifying solely with the qualities that match the sex of our bodies. It's really simple. So the point is to integrate the opposite sex archetype into our consciousness.

It makes total sense. We're only limiting ourselves to half a potential if we only allow ourselves to experience half of the energy of the universe. In the words of Bernard Wehr, the anima leads a man into exploring depths of feeling, relationships, and sensitivity. By integrating the anima, a man learns his feelings, learns how to be in a relationship, and learns sensitivity. The integrated animus leads a woman into the world of the spirit, leadership, and the power of the word or the ability to vocalize, her true voice. How powerful is that?

Integration of the anima and animus is portrayed in various texts as androgyny. Modern terms for androgyny include *metrosexual* or *ubersexual*. In modern times, we now refer to men who have accepted the feminine in themselves as metrosexual or ubersexual. (An ubersexual is a metrosexual who is low-maintenance while metrosexuals have become synonymous with being very high maintenance.) For women, the word expressing androgyny might be *independent*. An independent, empowered woman is the positive.

The other thing that I want to point out is that although we're talking about androgyny and being self-sufficient inside yourself, it doesn't negate having a relationship. My wife Soomi is an independent leadership-quality woman who would be fine whether I'm here or not. I'm totally comfortable nurturing my kids and I can dance a mean hula. Yet we've been in a relationship now for over 10 years. So it is possible to be in a relationship with someone who has resolved their animus or anima.

Integration of the anima/animus has been described as androgyny for many centuries. It is symbolized in tales and legends through the accomplishment of a special connection. Ancient Persian, Chinese, and Greek mythology had told of characters who had both male and female physical traits like the gods Aphroditus and Hermaphroditus. But most modern tales and myths play this special connection out as a relationship of the perfect man and perfect woman coming together in harmony, like the knight in shining armor who saves the beautiful maiden or Shrek saving the princess.

If you work out this anima/animus resolution through a relationship, meaning external, your partner can then become a conduit for you to understand your unconscious mind. When you have a *healthy* anima/animus projection onto the person with whom you're in a relationship, they then accurately reflect the beauty that is your unconsciousness. According to Jung and to Papa Bray this anima and animus is your unconscious mind. Again, if consciously you are a man, your unconscious mind is feminine. It is your anima. If you're a woman, your unconscious mind is animus or masculine. The anima or animus gets projected out onto another person.

However, in the person who is not in a relationship, the same thing occurs. The only difference is you open up a clear connection and channel between you and your unconscious mind rather than a partner. Free-flowing exchange occurs. For example, a student of mine, Mark, initially came to my workshops as a real guy's guy. He was somewhat stiff and definitely closed emotionally. But after several trainings, rather than finding the ideal female outside of himself, he started exploring the feminine inside of himself. He's now into hula and hugs, and is much more ready for a good relationship than he was before.

My ability to be with Soomi and not worry about how I look or how I act knowing she accepts me for who I am and vice versa, is a knowing that occurs internally. If you work from the angle of the relationship, that ability begins to then come into the self. And if you work from the angle of the self, that ability then goes into the relationship. As I began to work this aspect internally, it enhanced my relationship. So you can work on integration by either working with your partner to bring the anima or animus into balance in your relationship or by working internally to bring in those qualities of the opposite sex that had been suppressed into your experience.

In order to integrate your Shadow, you have to accept that you have thoughts and desires that do not fit your perfect image of the world. So the Shadow says, "I have my little perfect world. Everyone else is evil." To integrate the Shadow, we have to stop condemning those around us, withdraw our projections for those we condemn and accept them. We have to stop condemning ourselves as well. We have to understand those awful problems that we're trying to run away from may also have some meaning in our lives. That's Shadow. In my opinion, the Shadow is actually a little bit easier to process because there's something to learn from those nasty things that you see.

The relationship between the anima and the animus is a little more challenging because we're not dealing with our own personal unresolved material but the archetypical relationship between all men and women. It becomes an inner filter through which we view all relationships. With the anima and the animus, essentially you're having to deal with your own personal unresolved material along with the archetypical relationship between all men and women that has become the inner filter you use to view all relationships.

ANIMA/ANIMUS IN RELATIONSHIPS

When men and women fall in love, it's a total shock to the personal identity. All the rules fall away when two people come together in a typical relationship. Life only has meaning when they are with the lover or thinking about the lover. The lover is perfection itself beyond criticism.

Unfortunately, no person is that perfect. So within a short amount of time, reality begins to chip away at that little bubble of perfection. Just as no person is as evil as the Shadow makes them out to be, no partner is as magnificent as your anima or animus makes them out to be.

As with the Shadow or the anima/animus, we are projecting our inner opposite sex qualities onto someone else that just provides a hook. As the relationship develops, we actually see the person for who he or she really is. In the beginning, they seem perfect because everything that you have repressed that is your anima or animus, you have projected onto that partner. So they look like god or goddess. But within a short amount of time you begin to realize that he or she is not a god or goddess.

In many relationships in Western culture, the shock that the partner is not as perfect as you thought they were is enough to end he relationship. "You're not the person I thought you were." People who experience this frequently tend to jump from relationship to relationship to relationship.

Like a woman whose partner is "not strong enough, not vocal enough, doesn't have the leadership qualities." She leaves him and sees a man who seems to have those qualities. She gets hooked and gets together with him. "He's fabulous!" She really gets to know him and all of a sudden, he's not. Hook's gone. Next guy. Hook. Connects with him.

"Uh oh. He's not really Prince Charming." Hook's gone. Next guy. Hook.

While she's doing this, she may even feel a kind of déjà vu experience. In a sense, these guys were all the same. Technically they are because though they are different physical entities, they are the very same projection. If she had just stayed with one of them, she would have had the opportunity to actually explore her own need for the qualities she initially saw. By jumping from relationship to relationship, she never gets the chance to integrate her opposite sex qualities into her own personality.

Just as we saw with the Shadow, we need to stop projecting our anima and animus qualities onto the members of the opposite sex. It's not as easy to do with the anima and the animus. It is easier to do if you've done sufficient Shadow work.

If you've done sufficient Shadow work and arrived at the point where you've begun to resolve the Shadow, dealing with anima/animus is easier to do. Dealing with anima/animus is a little bit more difficult because with the anima/animus it's not who you despise. It's who you love. And because you love those qualities in your partner, you somehow want to leave them in your partner rather than integrating them into yourself. I often tell students that you wouldn't see those magnificent qualities that you see in your partner unless they were in you.

When we arrive at the source of the anima and animus, we gain an experience of our opposite. When you feel that hook and you link up with the anima and animus, you're really getting to explore the qualities of your unconscious. When you dig deep with the Shadow and resolve the Shadow, what happens is you see yourself looking back. When you dig deep with the anima and animus, you see your complement looking back.

As you begin to do Shadow work, you come to see yourself. When you do work with the anima and animus, the reflection is your complement. When I'd gotten really resolved on my anima, what I saw looking back at me was Soomi. I realized that I have the same qualities she has.

Although men and women unite, they nevertheless represent opposites, which are irreconcilable in the physical realm. Even when two come together intimately, there is still this aspect of opposite. That connection is just like in the yin yang symbol where you have the two, each within the circle and a dot within in each that is the color of the opposite. In a yin yang symbol that's drawn really well, you can see another yin yang within each dot. These smaller yin yangs each have a dot with a yin yang inside.

RECONCILING ANIMA/ANIMUS

Where to begin reconciling anima/animus? Sometimes, it's easy to start with mom and dad if you haven't yet reconciled them. Here's what you need to do: Actively imagine your ideal partner (even if that is your mom or your dad if you are starting from the original). It doesn't matter whether it's the person you're with or not. It can be someone who is fictitious, an ex, who you're currently with, or who you wish you were with.

When you have your ideal partner in mind, write down all of the qualities that he or she possesses that makes that person your ideal partner. Everything and anything that stands out. You might come up with qualities that are not as relevant as others, so rank them in order of importance.

Starting with the highest ranking word, notice where you actually exhibit that quality. Own it. Make it yours. Recognize that it is in you. Work your way down the list. If you hit a word and think, "I just don't have that quality," pay attention. This is what is known as a limiting decision. In addition, notice any negative charge you have with any of the qualities. Release any negative emotions around these words as in the *Keawe* process (page 46) or NLP chunking up process (page 30) (Also see Resources to order free MP3 download of these processes).

Owning Your Anima/Animus
- Write down the characteristics of your ideal partner.
- Prioritize in importance to you
- Beginning with the #1 characteristic, acknowledge that each ideal quality is within you
- If you meet with resistance, use chunking up or *Keawe* process to incorporate that quality

What do I mean by limiting decision? If as a woman, you think, "I can't be a leader because people will see me as being aggressive," that's a limiting decision. That's the ego getting in the way. That's the ego resisting the process. If you have any reason why you couldn't adopt the qualities you see in your ideal man, you've got to let go of any negative emotions, limiting decisions.

It's the same with men. If, as a man, you say, "I just couldn't do that because the guys would think that I'm a sissy if I had any emotion," that's a limiting decision, the ego resisting a part of the whole. When I tuck my son Ethan in good night, I give him a big hug and kiss. I know men who won't do that. They refuse to even hug their own son.

So, write down all those qualities that you find in your ideal partner whether it's a man or woman. This will work whether that ideal partner is an opposite sex partner or same sex partner. Find the qualities in your ideal partner and rank them in order. Note the ones that you don't believe are you, and let go of the negative emotions and limiting decisions using the processes mentioned above.

IS IT SHADOW OR ANIMA/ANIMUS?

Shadow is typically same sex. You meet the person; you want to kill them. When the charge is with the opposite sex, it's usually anima-animus issues. Shadow is typically the same sex because the Shadow is a projection of the ego and the ego identifies with whatever your sex is. If you're a man, ego identifies with being the man. You tend to project that.

Jung said that the anima-animus is the soul image, which is actually the opposite sex. Actually, anima-animus when it's unconscious usually shows up as a desire. Anima and animus is usually "I love that person." The anima/animus hook is that you desire them. The hook for the Shadow is that you hate it or fear something. For both men and women, the anima/animus hook is most often a positive reaction. But it can be a negative reaction from a suppressed anima and animus inside of you. You're seeing a quality that you actually really want but you're just angry about it.

I worked with a lady one-on-one years ago. She was irritated by guys who were all muscle-bound but dumb, meathead, masculine, macho. We chunked up one logical level, broadened the perspective. I said, "What is that an example of?" She says, "Health. Oh damn!" I said, "What?" She then explained that health was the issue she came to me to work on. So she was actually angry with her animus for being so healthy, which is what she herself wanted. That's not an unconscious animus/anima issue. In this case, it was a Shadow issue.

SOURCE

ANIMA / ANIMUS

COLLECTIVE / ARCHETYPE

HIGHER
SELF

CONSCIOUS
MIND

UNCONSCIOUS
MIND

SOURCE

ARCHETYPES

In between the anima and the animus and the self is what Jung referred to as archetypes. I'll start from the Huna perspective then I'm going to switch back to Jungian thinking.

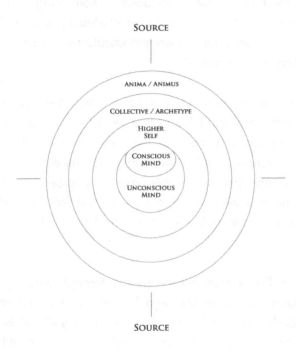

It's important to understand at this point where the archetypes are. In the dictionary, an archetype is defined as the perfect example of something, the original prototype from which all copies come. A lot of people talk about archetypes: the mother/father archetype, the Tarot, the Hero, the Wise Old One. What is an archetype in *Huna*? From the *Huna* perspective, an archetype is a more particular, specific representation within the two major archetypes: yin/yang, *Kane/Na Wahine* or anima/animus.

All archetypes, specific or abstract, reside in the unconscious. People use this term very loosely. But an archetype is your projection of what you think that person or type of person should be. Your projection can come from a variety of sources: your culture, family, religion, even the media. And archetypes can change. For example, the mother archetype, our societal expectation of what a mom should be, has shifted over the past 400 years. Those expectations are what Jung referred to as an archetype. It's the collective's viewpoint on something or someone. Haven't our female and male archetypes shifted even over the past 50 years? What the archetypical woman should be like and what the archetypical man should be like?

In other words, archetypes are not fixed. They are symbols that represent an epitome or model, and that model can be good or bad. For example, for many centuries, the devil in Western thinking represented the archetype of "all evil." When you have an archetypical response, it's where that aspect becomes your projection. In other words, if you find yourself trying to act as the "perfect mother" or the "courageous hero," it's more like a projection of what is housed in your unconscious.

An archetype is like a reservoir of energy through which you filter the world around you. Someone who believes that a certain group of people is a certain way and "that's just the way they all are" is filtering their experience through that generalized energy. The difference between a stereotype and an archetype is that a stereotype is much more conscious. I don't know that Jung ever dealt with the word "stereotype" but I feel pretty safe saying that Jung would say that a stereotype is an archetype that is more conscious and less transpersonal or spiritual.

But true archetypes are purely unconscious and, from both a Jungian and *Huna* viewpoint, collective. You can think of it in one of two ways: One is that it's a societal viewpoint that's imprinted on a child in years 0 through 7. During this time, the ideal archetypes are imprinted through the media, through parents, through family, through culture, religion, and various other influences. So by the time a child reaches a certain age, he or she has an archetypical viewpoint of how mom and dad should be.

The second way to think of archetypes is in energy terms. As I learned from Huna, there were two main archetypes: *Kane/Na Wahine*, which is masculine/feminine, not male/female. These two major archetypes are formless. They are energy. They are yin yang. They are masculine/feminine which is just raw energy. In contrast, though anima and animus are archetypes, you embody one physically and project the other out to a physical being. Man and woman is a physical expression.

Papa Bray believed that the two main archetypes, those two main energies, show up in different forms. Jung agreed but Papa Bray believed that it all goes back to anima/animus, and that if you're able to reconcile that, there is a trickle-down effect from the energy level into the physical. Papa Bray lived in a simpler society in Kona so it was easier to bring it back to anima and animus. Our Western society, however, is more complicated and we encounter a variety of archetypes that I think can be helpful on to you on your path.

MOTHER / FATHER

The first two expressions of anima and animus that you encounter are mother and father, and they are critical to your development. Mother and father are your first experience of the male and female, the two major archetypes, the anima and the animus. You look to one to see who you should be, and you look to the other to see how the other half of creation should be.

It's similar to your encounter with the anima and animus. When you first meet the anima or animus, there's a hook that draws you in. The mother and father are slightly different, in that we come into this life with an idea, energetically, that Mom should be a certain way and Dad should be a certain way. Depending on your belief system that idea could come from the collective or from universal energy or it could be a decision you've made through past lives through karma. It could be imprinted as you're growing up: You're seeing media. You're getting fed your values by your parents. Either way, as a child you are looking through a certain set of filters that makes your mom and dad seem like they are infallible and all powerful.

Even when Mom or Dad do something negative, from a psychological viewpoint, up to a certain age during a developmental period, a child looks up to the parent and aspires to be them. Even in a completely dysfunctional household – even if you now think, "No way could I have seen my father or mother as ideal!" – there was a point at which they were an ideal to you. They represented what Jung called the mother and the father archetypes.

What are some of the qualities we think of for the mother archetype? Nurturing. Caring. Compassionate. Emotional. We also have tangible expectations like mother can cook and bare children. In addition to the collective ideals, you also look at your own mom and say, "This is how a mom is supposed to be." And because "mother" is a specific example of the female archetype, at another level, you unconsciously adopt the idea that "This is what a female is supposed to be like."

At first, the mother and the father are lumped all together, because young children don't separate them clearly. But later, you identify with the one who shares your sex and you think, "This is how I'm supposed to be." At that time, you begin to form a different type of bond with the parent who is the opposite sex. In other words, as you begin to realize that you are female, your animus initially gets projected first onto the father. If you're a male, your anima gets projected onto your mother.

I think this is the basis of that old adage, "Men want to marry women who are just like their moms." You marry your father, you marry your mother. It makes sense from a Jungian perspective because that is where you got your initial information about anima/animus. This was especially true before TV invaded our homes 24/7. Before TV, the real-life people in the house were your family unit and they were the people you observed to learn about life.

But your relationship to the mother and father archetype changes. At some point as a child, usually during the modeling or socialization phase as an early teen or pre-teen, suddenly you look at your parents and think, "Dad's not as cool as I thought he was. He's actually a bit of a dork." Or, "Mom isn't as all-knowing or as nurturing as she once was." Or, "Her cooking actually sucks!"

By the way, it doesn't matter if your dad really is pretty cool or if your mom makes great food. I remember when I looked at my Mom's cooking and thought, " Really, Mom, again?" Of course, guess what dishes I'm cooking now? All those un-cool dishes Mom cooked. It's a cycle. I've become my Mommy.

The key here is that in a healthy, developmental, ideal path, that shining armor is chiseled away and the angelic halo fades. You see Mom and Dad for who they are and you no longer hold them to the standard you once had. You realize they're human, just like you, with all their flaws and mistakes and beauty and amazing qualities. And even if you think to this day, "I would never be like that," we've learned from the Shadow that we all carry that potential. If anything, mother and father demonstrated to you how to live your life and how not to be. You reconcile it, and your mother and father still are your mother and father. However, in a healthy development, you no longer punish them for not having lived up to your initial projection.

Many people hold on to being angry with their moms and dads for not living up to who we thought they should be when we were three. We're no longer three. Yet, that benchmark, our standard at three, is what we compare them to. Does that make sense? No. But the goal here is to recognize that while you were developing, they served a purpose: to show you anima/animus, to assist you in separating who you are from who you aren't.

I see that happening with my daughter Skylar already. She's in that 0 to 7 year old phase and she likes to watch me shave. She's so much like her mother. She won't give me a kiss if I haven't shaved. That's exactly what her lovely Mommy does. Daddy doesn't like to shave every day, because it sucks. But Skylar knows, by watching her mom, that "we'd really prefer it if Daddy shaved." She says, "No kisses, Daddy. It's too poky and dirty." The other day, she scratched my face then looked at me. "Will I have to shave Daddy?" I said, "No, honey. Only boys shave their face." Right there, I realized, in the best way I can, how I can empower her, yet at the same time help her differentiate between men and women. She's beginning to separate the two out. Of course, I didn't explain that she'd be waxing and plucking and doing all other kinds of things to get rid of hair! I'll leave that to her mom.

This is important because at one point, you are androgynous energetically. Oddly enough, that's what we're trying to get back to energetically. It's a full cycle. We start off as just a baby. We don't know whether we're a boy or a girl. Your parents know but until a certain stage, you don't.

The separation had begun for Skylar at that time. It began where she's realizing: "Oh, so I'm like Mommy. And my brother Ethan is a boy, like Daddy." There's the separation. Who do I identify with? Then, for her, I then begin to represent her animus.

Skylar's still at that age where Dad can do no wrong. She'll watch a fairy tale and she'll come running around the corner saying, "Daddy, I'm a princess. You're the King, come rescue me." I'm the king and I have to play that role, all the while knowing at one point that armor is going to come crashing off. So if you are a parent of a young child, enjoy it while it lasts. It doesn't last forever – and it shouldn't.

It's healthy to see your parents as actually being human at some point. Because that reconciles the mother and father archetype, which in a way, helps to make working with the anima and animus easier. And that's probably the most important part of working with the mother and father archetypes.

So at some point, it's healthy to be able to look at your parents and realize that who they are and how they behaved is part of you, part of your learning. We get stuck on, "Well, Mom could have done that better or Dad should have said that." We have all thought that way, haven't we? We forget that they were just human beings doing the best they could at that time. As we get older, we run into life and start realizing what adult human beings face every day and what our parents faced. It especially happens when you step into their shoes by becoming a parent yourself.

For example, I remember when my son Ethan broke his collar bone. There he was in the doctor's office in a sling. It was cute because he couldn't pronounce collar bone. He said, "I broke my colla' bone." It was so cute, but I'm still freaked because he was there in a sling, right? All of a sudden, I stopped and thought, "I remember when I broke my arm. I know how I feel now. I must have terrified my mom. To see me in the hospital, having a cast put on, the doctors not allowing her to come into the room at one point. I would have come unglued. No wonder she cried."

You stop for a second and realize, "Why they should be any better at dealing with stuff than we are?" They were just doing the best they could with the resources they had. You realize that you love them even more for that now, because you recognize they are just like you. They've got flaws, they've got cracks, they've got their idiosyncrasies. Yet your parents were able to help you get to where you are now in whatever way, shape or form they did it. That's reconciling the mother and the father archetype, when you realize you shouldn't hold them to any higher standard than you hold yourself.

It's not the easiest thing to do, especially from an astrological standpoint for those of you who have studied psychological astrology. From a projection, mother and father are at what astrologers call a hard angle. If you look at your houses, we project onto Mom and Dad at a square, which by its very nature makes it a hard angle energetically. It's difficult, sometimes, to reconcile. The mother and father are not opposing us, but they're not in a comfortable position by the time we come into our full maturity. There is a part of life's path where we need to learn and reconcile the fact that we've held them to a higher standard than we probably should.

How do you recognize when you have to deal with mother or father archetypes? It's when you still have a lot of should haves, could haves, and would haves about the past. "They should have done this." "They could have done that." "If only they would have said this or done that." Or maybe even thinking that your parents should be different in the present, that they should or could – if they only would.

What? Really? Here's one of the simplest tips. Are you ready? When you reach the same age where you remember your Mom and Dad and think they should have done or said something differently, stop for a moment. Ask yourself, "Do I have my act together so well that my kids will remember me as perfect?" If you don't have kids, pretend and add kids into the scene. Do you honestly think even those pretend kids will remember everything you did and said as brilliant?

I was 14 when my Dad was 40. I remember looking at him like he should have had his act together. But from my 40 year old perspective, I'm pretty clear that I don't have it all figured out. What standard was I holding him to? Why should I continue to do that now? Whatever answer you get, that's your own stuff. And don't get trapped in thinking, "But life was easier for them back then." No, it wasn't. That's all part of your projection.

So if you're still saying your parents "should have, could have, would have" about something in the past, or a present tense "should, could, would" if they're still with you, you have mother/father stuff to work on. The tip is that any answer you get about what they should have, could have, would have done is actually a lesson for you about what you should, could and ought to be doing now. Whatever you think they should have, could have or would have done, ask yourself if you are doing it. Because, what you're still hanging onto is probably something you haven't yet integrated into yourself. Something I have said for a while is that you cannot grow up until you stop blaming your mommy and daddy. As long as you blame them, you are still the kid.

This is a time where you have to take an honest reflection of yourself and say, "If my Mom were standing right here, what would I tell her she should have, could have, would have done?" If you're drawing a blank, congratulations! But if you do come up with some things, spend a little bit of time with them. Ask yourself, "What lesson do I need to get from it, and have I got the lesson?" It may not be a direct correspondence, a one-to-one connection between something specific you think your dad should have done and what you should be doing. It may be more like a general theme. Look at the entire list that you made and ask, "What is the lesson that I'm still clinging to, that I need to integrate?" Because, truly the lesson isn't ever for them. They are your projection. What you have done is make someone who is not an archetype live up to an archetype. You are trying to make your human parent live up to some ideal that was passed down energetically or from a collective.

To reconcile it, allow your mother and father to be who they are: your mother and father, no more, no less. You need to explore what it is that they should have been that they weren't, or aren't being that they should be only for the lessons you need to learn. You can get those lessons one of two ways: the direct correspondence and a more generalized learning.

A lot of times in my life, I found it was almost a direct correspondence. For example, I'm always checking email and whatnot. My son Ethan and I were together one weekend and I was about to say the words that I had heard growing up as a kid, "Hold on, Dad has got to work." I stopped and thought of how that was my biggest gripe growing up, that dad seemed to be always busy with work. So I said, "Okay, Ethan, here's your computer. Sit down. Let's do this together." We sat down and did it together, and that became a pattern. As a young boy, he used to say, "Dad, is it time for us to do homework together?" Now, his memories of me while he was growing up will definitely not be all great times and brilliant conversation. But at least his memories will include that, even when I worked, I brought him in.

I got the lesson from my own memories. I was about to do the exact same thing with my son that I'd experienced with my dad, and still hold on to blaming my dad for being the way that he was. To separate that lesson out was really freeing. It not only helped my relationship with my son, it also took a lot of heat off my Dad because I let him be who he is. That was a very one-to-one, direct correspondence lesson for me.

But if it's not a one-to-one direct correspondence, you have to look at the overall picture and ask yourself, "What is this an example of?" as in the NLP process of chunking up mentioned earlier (see page 30). Take specific incidents or memories and chunk them up by bringing them to a more abstract quality. That will give you perspective to find out what the lesson is for you from the mother and father archetype.

For example, my friend Heather grew up with a mother who worked very hard to make sure that family gatherings and celebrations were special. She watched her mom exhaust herself to create great decorations, prepare the perfect food, even set up games to make sure everyone had fun. But her mom never seemed to relax and enjoy the parties herself. As an adult, Heather started to notice that she didn't really feel comfortable in social settings. "I always felt awkward if I didn't have a job to do or role to fill. I was fine helping with the dishes or if I was in charge of greeting people. But just as a guest, hanging out? It felt weird." Finally, Heather recognized that her perfect mother archetype was always helping, arranging, in charge of events – never just a guest. By acknowledging this, she was able to relax and release herself from always being "on duty."

The overall lesson might be that your parents did the best they could. The key would be what you are doing with what they did now. Have you learned the lesson? It's not really about who your parents are or what they did. Sometimes this is really easy to grasp when you have siblings. Have you ever talked to your siblings and said, "I really wish Dad had done that." They look at you like you're crazy. "What you're talking about? Dad did that all the time." Your memories of the exact same household, the exact same mom and dad are totally different. Then you truly get an experience of the fact that it was your perception. The key isn't how to reconcile with that parent. The key is how you reconcile it in yourself.

You've got to get the learning. "What is the lesson? What is it that I wanted so desperately?" When you incorporate that lesson and bring it into how you live your life, you might do either one of two things: forgive your parent for whatever he or she did or didn't do, or actually see that they did it but in their own way. You have your way of doing life; they have a different way.

For instance, a classic example is expressing love. Your dad may have expressed his love by making sure he could put bread on the table. You may express love by hugs and kisses. Same love, different expression. Your way of expressing love is different and you feel good about it.

But if you're not expressing love in any form, you might still be focusing on him as having not expressed it, at least not in a way that made sense to you. Once you identify that lack in yourself, it's definitely time to forgive and release your parent.

I ran into another example of this with my mother. When I was growing up, my grandparents moved wherever my mom was to make sure someone was there to take care of the kids. My mom wants to live in California now. I lived in Honolulu and was almost ready to follow her so she could be close to my kids. Then I thought, "Wait a minute. I want to move to Kona. I want to live where I want to live. My mom is actually doing what I so desperately want to do. I want to move to the place I really want to live: Kona." And I did.

My mother's example had freed me. Previously, I had been quietly judgmental that she had moved us all to where she wanted to live. Yet it didn't really bother me until I was stuck not doing what she is actually doing right now: living where she wants to live. So what if my grandparents moved around to take care of us kids? My mom's behavior was the behavior that I needed to learn from.

I think when you resolve your mother and father archetype, even if they're still alive and in your life right now, you can see their behaviors and simply wonder, "What is there to learn from this?" It's no longer that they've got to live up to some standard. You see them as being human. A trick here is that you may have done a lot of work to release negative emotions in general, which is great. But it means that your sense of "should have, could have, would have" with your parents is more subtle, more cerebral. Even though there's not an emotional charge, it doesn't negate the fact that you have to deal with it, learn from it, integrate it.

What about grandparents? Grandparents are perfect, even according to Jung. I have a whole different take on grandparents. It's called

"Something shuts off in your brain when you become a grandparent." All parental cognitive thinking disappears. I caught my mom giving chocolate and soda to Ethan when he was about three – then telling him to lie to me about it! I'm looking at my mom thinking, "Should I put you in timeout?"

But here's the value of the parent-to-grandparent relationship. Having to deal with your parents as the grandparents of your children just takes you into the mother and father archetype again. It brings up anything that you haven't resolved. "Gee whiz, Mom, you didn't give me sodas until I was twelve!" It helps you go back into and release anything that's within the mother/father archetype. You recycle through dealing with mother/father issues again.

HERO

Two other major archetypes from a Jungian perspective were the Hero and the Wise Old One. The Wise Old One is actually the aim or the end result of the Hero's journey. The Hero archetype represents a person who has a calling or a desire, but isn't living his or her true life yet. The Hero then encounters some sort of falling down on the path, a loss if you would, that forces him to get started on whatever it is that he hasn't started on. And at that time where she falls, there is something or someone who comes along to help and pick her back up so she can get moving again. This is the Wise Old One. In my experience, the two – Hero and Wise Old One – are very closely tied together.

How often is that theme, the Hero's journey, presented to us from the time we were children? My daughter Skylar will recall the movie *Tinker Bell* forever, whether consciously or unconsciously. From my own childhood, I could easily use *Peter Pan*. I don't remember it as well as *Tinker Bell* because I haven't watched it 70,000 times like I've watched *Tinker Bell* with Skylar by now.

In the movie, Tinker Bell is created and the queen fairy brings her to life. Possible talents are presented to her, one of which is the tinker fairy talent. At first, Tinker Bell is okay with being a tinker. But then she realizes that tinker fairies don't go to the mainland. The water fairies do, the animal fairies do. But she has to stay there and just make pots and pans.

She has an experience of falling down on the path when she wrecks Spring. She wrecks the whole season! She screws up big time in trying to be something that she's not. She is "picked up" after falling down, not through a Wise Old One, but another fairy who is just a dust keeper. Tinker explains to him how amazing he is. And, but he says, "What? I'm just a dust keeper fairy." "But without you, the dust would not be able to allow us to fly."

Suddenly Tinker realizes, "I have this ability inside of me," and she saves the day. All by herself, she figures out how to save Spring. In the second movie she does it all over again. It's the same thing: she messes up then figures out that she has everything she needs to fix it inside of her. She breaks the crystal that has the fairy dust she needs. Actually, when you look at all of the Tinker Bell movies (which you probably won't bother to do unless you have a very young daughter!), they're all the same thing.

Another example is *The Matrix*. In that movie, Neo knows that there must be something more. He finds the Wise Old One, Morpheus. Neo falls down literally, physically. He has to rebuild himself. Morpheus continues to give him lesson after lesson after lesson, until Neo finally has to step out on his own and do what he is meant to do.

Luke Skywalker of *Star Wars* is another example. Remember the first scene where he is dreaming of something more looking out at the horizon? He loses everything. He finds his Wise Old One in Obi-Wan Kenobi. Darth Vader is another example of the Hero's journey because it is about the quest, not whether it's good or evil. Through our own Hero's journey, we may judge others. But in fact, Anakin Skywalker (Darth Vader) became exactly what he wanted to be. Now, Darth Vader was redeemed in the end to make everyone feel better. Personally, I think they should have just left him as James Earl Jones, the voice. But truly Darth Vader became who he wanted to be. He completed his Hero's journey. He found a Wise Old One in the Emperor to guide him and teach him his path, which was to become Darth Vader, adding a whole other layer of this valuable lesson.

Each journey is different but they all have the same theme. It starts with feeling that there is more to life. Next someone comes along who seems to have it all figured out and helps you get up to a certain point. But then he or she says, "Dude, you've got to do it on your own," either by saying, "I can't do anymore. You've got to figure it out," or by no longer being accessible as Obi-Wan was.

WISE OLD ONE

The Wise Old One is a key component of the Hero's journey and an important archetype so let's expand on that topic. As Dr. Robin Robertson said, the Wise Old One is not wise old man or wise old woman, because it transcends male/female. Something comes or someone comes along and is able to say, "Here, let me help you begin your path," which is the beginning of the journey of the Hero toward his or her purpose in life or to fulfill something.

This Wise Old One uses personal knowledge of people and experience in the world to offer guidance and encourage the Hero by embodying who he really is and who he might become. The Wise Old One acts as a mentor and is often mystical like Merlin in the King Arthur tales. The Wise Old One gives the Hero a broader perspective and might explain the significance of events within the journey.

By the way, you could argue that the Oracle was actually the Wise Old One in *The Matrix*. I wouldn't disagree with that. Morpheus actually archetypically played a stronger Wise Old One role. However, just like in a real life's journey, a Hero on the journey may encounter multiple individuals, all of whom play a role because the journey is cyclical. For Luke Skywalker, first there was Obi-Wan, then Yoda. He had progressed to another level: "I can stand on my own. I've destroyed the death star."

Another aspect of the Wise Old One: there is a natural transition of power. In storytelling, the character of the Wise Old One is often killed or disappears for a time to allow the hero to develop on his/her own. In my own life, Uncle George was there to say to me all the things I needed to hear and to be there when I needed him. When he had passed away, that was a great loss for me and many others. The first training I ran after his death, I felt like, "We've got to get Uncle back. Oh, my goodness, we need him. What would I do without Obi-Wan Kenobi?" "No Yoda, you can't die. You have so much more to teach me!" You begin with the belief that you don't have all of it. But in truth, what you see in that person, the qualities or wisdom you think you need from the Wise Old One, you have it all within yourself. For a time, the other person is the Wise Old One. Then suddenly you realize that you're the Wise Old One. "I'm living the lessons that I was seeking from him or from her."

In some paths, for example in *The Matrix*, the Wise Old One, Morpheus, doesn't leave. He didn't die or disappear. Instead, Neo turned around and helped Morpheus so the two of them could continue their journey together. Gandalf in *Lord of the Rings* is another example of the Wise Old One. He transforms and gets to a new level, but he's still on his journey. The Hero's journey is told in so many different ways because it is a very personal experience expressed in so many different ways. The Wise Old One can transform into new lessons.

You may see the person who is the Wise Old One and think, "I learned everything I need to learn." He has no more to share now or she has no more to teach me now. At that point, you've begun to develop those qualities inside yourself. You begin to have an aim and you're on your own journey knowing, "Here's where I want to go. I know I want to go that way because here's who or what I am seeking to help me move there, to help me get there." You may find a new old wise one at that point.

YOUR HERO'S JOURNEY

Why does the hero's journey so resonate with us all? Why does it show up so often in novels or movies? It's because it is the story of what we are meant to do in our lives. In fiction, it shows up as much more grandiose with all the boring parts left out and better special effects. But the Hero's journey really is the lesson of every human life. It is what astrology refers to as living out your solar journey or your solar path. It's learning how to stand in your own light so that you shine.

So let's define what it means to be the Hero, to stand in the light. I think this is the most important point. The hero who stands in the light has reconciled her persona, ego, the Shadow and is now connected with higher self and is fully *pono* with who and what she is.

In all of these examples that I've given you, the Heroes have to reconcile their projections to become fully who they are meant to be. I remember Neo in *The Matrix* protesting to Morpheus, "But the Oracle told me I wasn't the one." Morpheus cut him off and said, "The Oracle told you exactly what you needed to hear at that moment." The Oracle never actually said, "You are not the one Neo." The Oracle said, "What do you think?" And Neo responded, "I'm not the one," so the Oracle said, "Bingo. You have to believe it to be it." She never said, "You're right Neo, you're not." But Neo perceived it that way based on his projections. He ended up dying later and became the chosen one!

So what does the Hero's journey look like in real life? It's you in this journey that we are talking about right now. It is learning how to stand in your own light in your own way. Life is that journey. Staying on the sidelines doing nothing will only cause some event to come along to give you a kick start to get you on your hero's path.

For example, years ago I used to co-teach *Huna* with my father. I was happy being second fiddle with less responsibility. I tell you the life of being someone else's assistant for me was a life of luxury. I would go out, do the opening performance, do a little chanting, shake my hips around. I'd come in, release a couple negative emotions, go out, hang out and sit with Uncle George.

Someone even asked me during that time, "When are you going to start running your own trainings?" "Run my own trainings? What, are you kidding me?" I was avoiding my Hero's journey – and that's exactly when the Shadow shows up. You're avoiding whatever it is and yet deep down inside you know, "Oh, maybe one day."

Part of the Hero's journey and one of its lessons is that the longer you delay, the more energy you put into it. You could look at it from a Shadow perspective. One of the things about the hero's journey is that if you are not living out who you are meant to be, all you do is build up a lot of baggage and get a swift kick in the behind. I call that a behind because that's where you get kick-started to be forward, I guess. I don't know.

So the Hero is you and the journey could be many things. A journey can be learning how to become a great parent or how to become a good child. We sometimes diminish our own path and view it as unimportant because we aren't saving lives and we can't stop bullets and we don't have a bag of Tinker fairy dust we can sprinkle on ourselves.

These stories of Heroes' journeys have been told so many times and look so huge that they appeal to the unconscious. The unconscious understands that the Hero's journey is about all of us. But consciously, we just don't think it applies to us. We never sit back and consciously ask, "What does this mean to *me*?"

Here is what it means to you: you have to look at your path and realize that journey is as important as any of these other ones that you have ever seen or heard. The key isn't to look at a movie or another person's path and say, "I like that movie or path better. I'm going to make my Hero's journey that." The key is to figure out, "How am I going to get started on my journey? How am I going to begin to live it? And when I seek something or someone out, what am *I* looking for?"

It is a worthwhile journey. You will create the people who help you when you need to create them. And when you no longer need them, they will transform and take on a new role, whether by leaving or by their saying, "I have no more lessons to give you." Or it might even be by your saying, "It's time to move to a new phase." However it looks, the journey is important because it is yours.

The key to the journey is twofold. First, live your journey. You have to actually begin to know, "It is a journey. It is something that I'm going to do and it is worthwhile doing." It may not be grandiose. It is your journey, though. So you need to become pono with the fact that you need to do it.

And the second key is to realize that people come into your life who play the role of the archetype, the Wise Old One. You need them because you haven't yet owned the qualities that they present to you. At an unconscious level, the Wise Old One is a reflection of what you are aiming for, either literally or metaphorically.

You will have journeys in different parts of your life like your career, your relationships, your spiritual path. Think of the Hero's journey in every context of your life. Not only are there multiple journeys, at some point they begin to converge together. They begin to merge together, and this is a great point about the Hero's journey. Some point after you've run a few of these journeys, you suddenly realize, "There's a bigger theme here." That bigger theme is the point of all I've been talking about: It is connecting with the Self, self-empowerment.

I personally think you really have two different approaches to this. It's either do the Hero's journey in each context – only to realize it was the same thing that you just had to do in another context – or do the journey as an overall lesson and allow it to begin to express in every area of your life. One may be easier for you than the other.

For example, if you live a vastly different spiritual life than your career, you may have to experience the lesson in each context separately. It's not to say you cannot be spiritual within your career. I'm afforded something very unique in that I get to practice and teach and go home to exactly what I teach. You might be thinking, "I wish the areas of my life were all tangled up like Matt." Sometimes I wish it wasn't.

For example, I remember being on a car ride home with my then 10-year-old son who had just taken my class on the *Huna* assumptions. My normal car ride home is usually pretty meditative, which I like after talking for 11 hours straight. But Ethan had bunches of questions and talked the whole time. Who am I supposed to be then? His *kumu* (teacher) or his dad? I've had some people say to me, "Well, Matt it must be so easy to be working and living with your family so all six areas are just one big bucket of happy." Well, it's great and it's not great. But it's my journey.

But for you, you might have a Hero's journey in your career. You might have a Hero's journey in your family, a Hero's journey in your relationship, a Hero's journey in your spirituality, your personal growth, your health and fitness. And you travel along each one to find the overall theme that brings you closer to self. Either way, separate or merged together, is perfectly okay. There was a time in my life where things were separate enough that I did have to do the journey in one specific area by itself to help that area become grounded, to find my foundation there.

The Hero's journey is a cyclical experience because as soon as you get to a point where you think, "Okay, I got it," then you're right back at the beginning of the Hero's journey again thinking, "I'll just kick back here and sit on my behind." But really that's just the beginning of the next journey. It never ends. It's an aim, not a destination or an end.

RESOURCES

Please contact us to order your free MP3 download of:
- Huna & Ho'oponopono 1
- The Keawe Process

Or to purchase the CD collection:
- Introduction to Hawaiian Huna (10 CDs) $199.00*

Shipping charges apply and price subject to change

Advanced Neuro Dynamics, Inc.
75-6099 Kuakini Highway
Kailua-Kona, HI 96740

Toll free: 800.800.MIND (6463)
Phone: 808.791.5050

NLP.com
info@NLP.com